HANDLE
WITH
CARE

'Shreya's desire for new experiences, and her attention to detail, remind me of Robert Louis Stevenson's travel writings. Never a dull moment!' – RUSKIN BOND, AUTHOR

'I feel a deep personal connection to this book. Gerald [Durrell] always told me that one of the reasons for his family's move to Corfu was that his mother, Louisa, missed India terribly. She had been born, married and brought up children there, relocating to England only because of the sudden death of her husband. In the grey, damp and cold, she pined for the vibrant sights, sounds, scents and tastes of India, for the company of a warm and generous people, and the vivacity and colour her life had once had. Corfu, so like India in these many ways, rekindled her love of living.

'In this book we're immersed in India, Corfu and all other points of the compass, the author skilfully guiding our way and revealing the treasures that each and every place surely has. But above all, this is a book about love – romantic, parental, familial and whatever the word is for the family dog. About love of place, history, literature, poetry and art, all around the world. It celebrates adventure and fun. In short, it is totally wonderful, written lustrously, wittily and kindly, and I recommend it as a fabulous read for everyone, anytime, anywhere.' – LEE DURRELL, AUTHOR, NATURALIST, AND TV PRESENTER

HANDLE
WITH
CARE

TRAVELS WITH MY FAMILY
(To Say Nothing of the Dog)

To Arlenys,
Happy reading!

SHREYA SEN-HANDLEY

Best,
Shreya

HarperCollins *Publishers* India

First published in India by HarperCollins *Publishers* 2022
4th Floor, Tower A, Building No. 10, Phase II, DLF Cyber City,
Gurugram, Haryana – 122002
www.harpercollins.co.in

2 4 6 8 10 9 7 5 3 1

P-ISBN: 978-93-5489-316-2
E-ISBN: 978-93-5489-317-9

Cover design and illustration: Devangana Dash

Typeset in 11/15.2 Bembo at
Manipal Technologies Limited, Manipal

Printed and bound at
Thomson Press (India) Ltd.

𝐟 𝐢𝐧 ◎ 𝐲 HarperCollinsIn

MIX
Paper
FSC FSC® C010615

This book is produced from independently certified FSC® paper
to ensure responsible forest management.

To *my* family and other animals (because for this book,
only a Durrellesque dedication would do!)

Contents

1. Kolkata Durga Pujas: Armed and Marvellous   1

~ *Pause for Thought: Finding Magic in the Mundane*   7

2. London: Night at the Museum   10

3. Gotham: Batman's Lair   14

~ *Pause for Thought: Ponchos Aren't Forever*   19

4. Delhi and Rajasthan: The Golden Veggie Triangle   22

~ *Pause for Thought: Travelling as a Twosome*   36

5. Corfu: Garden of the Gods   39

6. Amsterdam: Sex, Drugs, and Sunflowers   49

~ *Pause for Thought: Going Solo*   55

7. Zurich: Moo-ving On   58

8. Sheffield: Nerves of Steel   64

9. Nottingham: Second Chances in Sherwood   70

~ *Pause for Thought: Qualities of a Tripfella*   74

10. New York and Las Vegas: Lady Liberty   76
~ *Pause for Thought: Stop and Smell the Kaapi*   84

11. Odisha and Kerala: Southern Comfort   87

12. Manila: Call of the Sea   99
~ *Pause for Thought: The Best Exotic Literary Tour Company*   108

13. England and Wales: The Game Is Afoot   110

14. Dorset: Four Go Off in a Caravan   117

15. Haworth: Wuthering Heights   124
~ *Pause for Thought: Tots Can Trot*   128

16. Wales: Train to the Top   132

17. Disneyland, Paris: Never Never Land   138
~ *Paws for Thought: Our Canine Conundrum*   146

18. Wye Valley: Puppy Love   151

19. Whitby: The Wet Dog in the Night-time   159

20. Travelling in India: Horn OK Please   168

21. Hong Kong, Bangkok, and Oman: Schoolgirl Errors   178
~ *Pause for Thought: Gallivanting with a Gaggle*   186

22. Nainital: The One with Friends   189

23. London: Orf with Their 'Eads   200

24. Nepal: The Hills Are Alive   207

~ *Pause for Thought: A Plan for All Seasons*   215

25. France in Summer: Le Grand Prix   218

26. Cambridge in Early Spring: The Queen's Gambit   230

27. Britain in Winter: Christmas Chronicles   235

28. Kolkata in the Monsoon: Homecoming Joys   242

~ *Final Pause: No Place Like Home ... However Many
Places That Might Be*   251

Acknowledgements   255

Sources   257

1

Kolkata Durga Pujas
Armed and Marvellous

There is magic in the air in Kolkata tonight. The autumnal night sky is lit with rainbow hues. These colours reflect off the pandals, those magnificent, glittering, multicoloured marquees. Tonight, our pandal-hop starts from south Kolkata's Selimpur and ends at Park Circus. The Gariahat road on which we walk is long and busy. We see hundreds of pandals, big and small, all decked up as distinctively as can be. We spot everything from a giant-bird marquee to the slightly less fantastical South Indian temple. We stop at a pagoda-like one in Ballygunge. It is stately, not serene. Nothing is serene during the Pujas. Though the air is filled with loud music and voices, the pagoda is worth a halt and deserves a better look. But that's precisely our problem. We – two little children and their diminutive mom – don't think we will get that better look tonight. In fact, close to the ground as we are, even the magic in the air slightly eludes us. Air itself does too, hemmed in as we are by a large, surging crowd, jostling and jabbering.

'Oh, Mommy,' said my seven-year-old daughter, 'it's bootiful, but I can barely breathe.'

It was clearly time for the Himshim Manoeuvre. Similar to the Heimlich Manoeuvre, Himshim brings release from a peculiar kind of choking particular to Kolkata at Pujo-time. I was about to find out if I'd grown rusty from my many years away. Gripping my children's hands tightly, I ploughed through the palaver of people till we breathed refreshingly un-regurgitated air on a quieter side street. There were enough people there still to fill a small hall, but it was undoubtedly easier to breathe. Soon spirited home in our car down similar back streets, the children were relieved but also eager for more. 'Shall we do it again?' asked our young man of nine.

Of course we would! That's why we were in Kolkata for the Pujas after twelve long years. We visited annually but till this year, the kids had seemed too young to enjoy the colour and chaos of the Pujas to the full. And much like the Goddess Durga's own homecoming, as celebrated by the Pujas, this was meant to be a triumphant one. We weren't meant to scuttle away after a single attempt at rubbernecking. We had not covered ourselves in Pujo-hopping glory on our first foray into the festivities. I was, however, determined not to be deterred by a puny crowd of thousands. Did Durga down arms and slink away when confronted by the macho Mahishasura? No, she grappled him to the ground instead. And so would I, I decided, find a way to master the Pujas all over again, introducing its magic and mayhem to my eager young 'uns in the most painless way possible.

I could no longer, I had to admit, flow through crowds like Saraswati's swan through water, or match Ganesh's nose for the finest grub. This time around, for example, it took a while to find the most mouth-watering double-chicken-egg rolls at the resplendent Park Circus Puja, which would have been the work of a mere few practised seconds years ago. Yet, some things hadn't changed. The enthusiasm was still there, as was the pluck. Most of all, the mind ticketh over as before. It was formulating a plan with the practicality of Lakshmi and the maternal instincts of Durga. And that all-conquering arsenal in the latter's ten powerful arms? I would need those too. Just adapted to less epic requirements to help me navigate, in feeble NRI ishtyle, this once-familiar festival:

❖ First of all, I'd need the goddess's three eyes. All the better to see the Pujas with. Our plan was to stick to familiar but spectacular south and central pujas near our Kolkata home on this trip, venturing farther north to take in more traditional beauties on the next. Within the span we set ourselves, we chose Mudiali for its glitz, Jodhpur Park for its ingenuity, and Maddox Square for its fashionable folk, of course. The second eye would help me watch the children, no matter how firm a hold I had on them at the time. And the third one, with a 360-degree sweep, would keep tabs on the insistent peddlers and even more persistent pinchers (of bags and other 'b' words).

❖ Then I'd need a conch. The goddess's conch blasting
out a primordial 'Om' apparently created whole
universes. Mine would just need to drown out the
cacophony of loudspeakers. Not only when we
were out Pujo-trawling, but all the time. Whether at
home with family, digging into autumnal delicacies
like malpoas and kosha mangsho, or in the thick of a
meaty adda, there are always PA systems blaring for
the Pujas. But though my conch would have to out-
boom those speakers, it mustn't drown out the dhakis,
the traditional drummers beating a rhythmic tattoo
through the festival. The rousing beat of the dhakis is
simply divine and no Pujo could be complete without
them. The best of them at a modest puja in Gol Park
made my heart and my children dance, and the conch
was forgotten.

❖ Along with the goddess's three eyes, you'd want her
trishul or trident. Because what's the point of being
all-seeing if you can't be all-doing as well? One
prong of which in our more humdrum not-creating-
universes sort of way could be a nimble DSLR to
take phenomenal pictures of the Pujas. Of the always-
elegant Ekdalia, the often splendid-in-a-tight-space
Dhakuria, or the incandescent College Square (not in
south Kolkata, I know, but an old favourite). Or you
could have a nifty (and tightly-clutched) smartphone
instead that not only takes photos, but gives you
directions when lost, which you're bound to get,
with every street changed beyond recognition by the

beautification and the barricades. The second prong could be the water bottles and stash of 'bishkoot' you plan to keep with you for the kids. When stuck in a traffic jam in between pandals as you invariably will be, Marie bishkoot or 'Kerackjack' will keep them occupied. The third and final prong of your trishul would have to be for despatching pests of all kinds — the ones you've identified with your omniscient third eye. Then your trident and your mace (a lot like the Devi's, except it works like a spray) will make short work of them.

❖ The deity's sword would come in handy too. It signifies a sharp intellect, and you certainly need to be able to think on your feet when out and about on a blazingly beautiful but busy Pujo night. In fact, with children, afternoons and even early mornings are much better for unimpeded viewing. We found smaller, back-alley pandals to be far more child-friendly. The children were blown away by the peacock marquee in Lake Gardens, and couldn't bear to leave the Fern Road pandal with its illuminated and animated animals. The friendliness of these parar pujos with locals warmly and personally ushering us in, added immeasurably to the experience.

❖ Don't forget Durga's bow and arrow either, symbols of energy, of which you'll need oodles for a proper pandal-crawl through even a quarter of Kolkata. Because when the sublime sculptors of Kumartuli get together with the masters of illumination from

Chandannagar and the inspired pandal-makers from all over the city, there is very little you'd want to miss, even if you have to run the gauntlet of all of Bengal to do it.

❖ You really will require the Devi's thunderbolt to light your way through those very crowds. And to create the occasional diversion when you want to manoeuvre the kids to the front because no amount of craning will allow them to see. Of course, keen night vision like that of Lakshmi's owl would help too, to savour the splendid sights while sidestepping the decorously covered potholes. Add to that Durga's inextinguishable flame, emblem of knowledge (which is precisely what I didn't have on that first foray into the Pujas as an outsider), and I'm all set.

Well, almost. We can't ignore her fearsome lion. Or my pair of cubs, less fearsome but as keen to get going. They are what this trip back to the motherland at this time of the year is about. With a firm grip on them and my good sense, taking care to stay stocked on all kinds of supplies, practical and metaphorical, I am ready to introduce them to the magic of the Durga Pujas. To the delight of dancing lights, delicious festive food, and that magnificent array of awe-inspiring pandals and majestic idols, that only Kolkata at Pujo time can provide.

Pause for Thought: Finding Magic in the Mundane

That was four years ago. It is summer now in Kolkata. The fans are whirring, moving the hot air around inside the house, which pursues the inmates as they dive, relieved, under showers and fans. Outside, the streets are baking in the sun, with what little vegetation there was on the edges wilting like the people crammed into flats. Ordinarily, the slow summer months would have slid into a crisp autumn, and then in a flurry of colour, artistry and energy, the eagerly awaited festivities – the Durga Pujas – would have arrived. We have flight tickets to be there this year too, but we don't think we'll make it in the middle of this most unexpected pandemic.

'All this will be over in a few months,' Didou declares, with a certainty I know she doesn't feel, on our twice-weekly video conference with them (made more frequent by the lockdown). My mother, the children's maternal grandmother in faraway Kolkata, is just as anxious as we are about the terrible situation the world finds itself in. Yet, October is a long way away, and things might indeed improve in time. Till then, the good memories of our last visit to Kolkata will keep both the children and their grandparents happy. 'The fish fry and mishti doi will be waiting for you, whenever you can join us next,' their Dadu, my father, reassures. 'And boy, is it going to be a shock to our systems after the solitude of these months!'

'A shock indeed. But our holidays are always full of surprises,' I chortle with the two children and our dog, when the videocall is done. 'Even the ones that give us a jolt, where something unexpected and not entirely pleasant happens, can be fun in retrospect. Ones to remember!'

'We've had all sorts of mishaps on holiday, haven't we?' The son giggles at the memory.

'But wouldn't dispense with any of them,' I finish for him.

As an everyday family, striving to keep ends neatly tied in every situation, including holidays, even as we manage to enjoy it all a great deal, very little that we do goes to plan. It will rain, or we'll get lost, or fall sick, or something surreal will happen. That's not because we overreach with our holidays, not at all; we have modest ones. With the exception of our one long trek to India every year, they are neither expensive, nor extravagant, or extreme in any way.

We are, as I said, just an ordinary family of five. My husband Steve is in finance, has a beard, wears glasses, and sings out of key. But he also cooks marvellously, photographs with flair, fixes every seemingly insurmountable problem, and is our rock. The daughter is a bright spark, rebellious but creative, loving and buoyant, while the son, our exceedingly stubborn deep-thinker, is both quiet and fun. As for the dog, well, the dog is daft, but adorable and full of boundless energy. And I? You'll get to know me as we go along. Together we make quite the quirky clan, living on the edge of Nottingham, in green and shady Sherwood Forest.

Except for those interludes in the year, when we strike out beyond the forest for our adventures in the world. 'We always find magic when we do,' the daughter exclaims, her face lighting up as she remembers the many enchanted sojourns we've been fortunate to have over the years. 'It's almost as if it follows us,' the young man agrees. We know it's nothing we knowingly do. We don't stretch our pockets, or even ourselves sometimes, except in the most gentle, pleasurable, inconspicuous way. But out of that unique maelstrom that make up our holidays, emerge the unexpected and the marvellous. While I reckon it is the frisson between us all that makes it so fabulous, the children, including the dog, believe it's something in the forest. Luna, our pup, certainly dashes into its green thickets often enough in search of this benevolent presence.

Because the near at hand can indeed be magical, especially when it is close to the heart. And that, you might say, is our philosophy – in life as in travel.

2

London

Night at the Museum

'Is that a raptor snoring?' our seven-year-old daughter asked wide-eyed.

Waking in the dead of night to thunderous snores reverberating around us, I couldn't immediately remember where I was. My nine-year-old son was on the ball though. 'Raptors aren't big enough to snore like THAT. It's gotta be a T-Rex!' Not far from the row of gigantic fossils behind which we'd settled for the night, there was indeed something loud, and quite possibly very large, snoring. And it wasn't Daddy because he'd been woken by it too. Nor had we breached a gap in the time–space continuum and travelled back to the Cretaceous Period. Or been magically transported to Conan Doyle's *Lost World* or the blockbuster *Jurassic Park*. Looking up, I could see the humongous skeleton of a more modern leviathan – the blue whale that had washed up on English shores in 1891 – taking up most of the vaulted ceiling of our vast bedroom for the night, and it all came back. We were participating in 'Dino Snores', a sleepover event at the Natural History Museum in London, home to 800 million species spanning 4.5 billion years on earth. Designed to teach kids about the natural world in a new and interesting way, it was certainly working because, shaken from our sleeping bags by locomotive-like rumblings in the magnificent Hintze Hall in the early hours, we now knew that dinosaurs definitely snored!

On a torch-lit tour earlier that night, we'd learnt another pack of eye-opening facts about them. Again, in the most unexpected way. After togging up for the adventure with dino T-shirts we'd designed on site, we struck out on the trail of the mystery dinosaur we were instructed to find. Armed with paper to note down clues, and a crayon each to defend ourselves, we walked through the darkened halls guided by torchlight. It wasn't long before we were hoovering up the clues and gathering the facts we'd been told to, expecting to scoot back to base in no time, and congratulating ourselves on a job nearly done.

No spooky skeleton or fearsome fossil – and we'd brushed past plenty – was going to stop us acing our mission. The clearly extinct and obviously fossilized don't frighten us, we laughed as we went. In fact, we oohed with delight when our torchlight found an imposing, 135-million-year-old iguanodon, and we aahed in wonder when our beam alighted on an astoundingly tank-like triceratops. But then something went bump in the night. Something that sounded distinctly alive. Our flashlights wobbled to a halt on a blinking eye, and then on the razor-sharp talons clawing the air a mere hair's breadth from us! It was scaly. It was screeching. It was one of those rapacious raptors!

It was also a robot, we realized quickly. One of the several animatronic dinosaurs scattered through the museum. We gave it a wide berth regardless, only to back into one that chittered greedily in our ears. Careful not to stumble into any of the other large lizards, especially those that seemed to be monitoring our every move, we arrived at our last set of clues. The mystery dinosaur of our quest turned out to be an enormous, roaring, foot-stomping T-Rex, filling the room as only the king of dinosaurs can. It seemed to take a swipe at us in the semi-darkness, making our entire torch-lit tribe jump. Then, with a gnashing of large, glinting teeth and wild swerves of its gigantic head, the fifteen-foot creature appeared to advance on us. And though everyone knew it was a robot and fixed to the floor, as a body we decided it was time for that king-sized snack we had been asked to bring along.

But enthusiastic as we were, many of us were not spring oviraptorosaurs any more, and we woke the next morning with aches and pains worthy of explorers. Yet, while my husband and I felt as if our old bones had been tested and bested by thin mats and those disturbingly thick snores, the children were raring to go. We found ourselves sitting campfire-style around a tottering pile of large boxes for one last communion with critters. And this bunch was very definitely alive. From furry friends like meerkats and South American chinchillas, to creepy crawlies such as African tarantulas and scaly slitherers like a young but already formidable boa constrictor, the man in charge trotted them out, one after another, to the delight and occasional horror of the hundred-strong crowd of children. Very few got the opportunity to touch, some more got to eyeball up close, but every kid learnt something new that day. As well as the night before. But amidst the lessons, the drama, and the comedy, a little swirl of mystery clung to our experience. Whose were those earth-shaking snores after all?

3

Gotham

Batman's Lair

'Goat-ham, Ma'am?'
I looked around wildly. I could have sworn I had
stepped into a newsagent's shop and not a butcher's. The
racks of newspapers and magazines, the high shelves of alcohol
and cigarettes, and for the children wandering in, a freezer of
ice-lollies, were all there. But no Mr Freeze. No Penguin. And
surely the farthest thing from the Joker was the man behind
the counter.

'Not GoTHam, but Goat-ham,' he grimaced. 'Goat town
is what it means. You won't find Batman here. Nor adventure.
It's a quiet English village.'

Quite another crime-fighting icon, Miss Marple, might
have had something to say about the dark and dangerous things
that happened in little English villages, I thought, as I stepped

out with the children into the mellow autumn sunshine. But it was the caped rather than the cardiganed crusader we hoped to spy in the foxglove-filled nooks and green-wreathed lanes of this Nottinghamshire village.

The sign on this shop definitely said *Gotham* News. So had the totem pole-like signpost that had greeted us as we drove in. A spiralling blue and gold tribute to the legendary denizens of this hamlet, it also had Batman climbing up its metallic side. It was true, I declared to the children, as I took their hands firmly in mine and marched down the deserted street, that there wasn't much evidence of mayhem in these parts. But Bill Finger, Batman's co-creator, hadn't named his fictitious anarchic metropolis after this English parish for nothing. And I knew just where to find the clues.

Strolling through the village, we came to a halt outside the jauntily lopsided Sun Inn, its neat olive-green shutters in sharp relief against a blue-washed sky. But across the street, in the protective shadow of Gotham's thirteenth-century church with its soaring spire, was what we'd come to see…

'Daddy!' the children pointed to the man loping towards us, who, having parked the family car, rejoined our promenade to the Victorian Well House. Recently restored with the help of Batman fans, I suspected this structure would prove to be the repository of the answers to the Gotham conundrum.

Inside were the only two people roaming Gotham's streets with us that afternoon, unmistakeable in their identical homage hoodies and rapt expressions. As our children's capes (but of course they were dressed the part!) fluttered in the wayward breeze that had wheedled its way into the modest edifice, we helped them onto the old stone plinth at its heart. And KAPOW! We were in GoTHam at last.

On the angled wooden ceiling was Batman himself. Or a picture, but one that seemed to swoop down with its black batwings outstretched. The children reached up reverentially, following the timeline that wound its way around the ceiling and walls with their fingers till they reached more intriguing legends still.

Here was American author Washington Irving, with his quill poised to link Gotham to New York for the first time in 1807, having read about the 'wise men of Gotham' and finding instant parallels with the bedlam of the Big Apple. New York embraced this new moniker with its implication of a cunning madness with gusto, and soon, there were businesses named after it mushrooming in their city. There, garlanding the cupola, were murals depicting the madness of the village residents. Village rabble rolling a wheel of cheese down a hill, another horde pooling round a pillar were planning to drown an eel, while the third yokel band tried their hand at fishing the moon's reflection out of the parish pond.

A century later, Bill Finger ran precisely that limb through business names in a New York phone book to find an appellation for his own mad, made-up city. Gotham first featured as Batman's home in December 1940. If Finger was aware of the name's antecedents, he may not have known just how wise Gotham's madness had been, as the villain of *The Batman Chronicles* of 1996 proves when he explains how he christened an asylum 'after a village in England where all are bereft of their wits'.

'But in fact they weren't,' the children's father told them, finally unravelling the mystery of the 'mad' folk of Gotham. 'King John, on his journey to the north of England, wanted to build a road through this peaceful village. A big public road. Naturally, the villagers, of sturdy Middle English stock, were having none of it. A public road would involve paying taxes after all!'

'So what did they do?' wondered our daughter, twirling on the plinth, the cape clouding around her darkly.

'How does one deter an all-powerful king?' I picked up the thread of the story as long shadows stretched in tiny Well House. 'The villagers colluded to frighten the king with the one scourge medieval monarchs feared more than the plague – madness! In the thirteenth century, insanity was not only considered a supernatural affliction but also infectious. So, when the soldiers came tramping through their land, the villagers, en masse, pretended to be as mad as March hares. Even tying their hard-earned purses to actual hares which then hared off, demonstrating how comprehensively they had lost their senses.'

'That is pretty mad,' grinned our son, patting his capacious pockets to ensure his pocket money was intact.

'But you know what's really mad?' I laughed. 'Fencing a cuckoo in a bush to keep it singing beyond the summer – look!' As their eyes followed my finger to the mural overhead, their dad interjected, 'But madder still would be a pit stop at the pub of the same name to refuel before returning home!'

We had all seen the red-bricked Cuckoo Bush, with its scarlet sign swinging in the wind like a gibbet, on our way up to Well House. As we ambled back, with the world darkening around us, we could hear peals of laughter through the latticed windows. Then the lights sprang on inside, and we saw for the first time the revellers within: a portly man in a black bow tie threw back his head and guffawed at what the feline woman beside him had to say. While, by the window nearest us, sat a man in a tall green hat, stroking his abnormally long chin and contemplating ... I now realized ... us!

'Did you see that?' I breathed, turning to my family to find them gone. They were running across the deserted street, their capes streaming after them, their masks failing to conceal the laughter swathing each face. 'There are more mad men who pass through Gotham than live within it,' the children cackled when I caught up with them in the car park. 'But,' I spluttered, as their father turned the car around to take us home, 'how did you little monkeys manage *that*?'

Pause for Thought: Ponchos Aren't Forever

'Do you remember your silly spat with your uncle over those godly treks he forced us on when we toured Rajasthan in your early teens? You were such a hothead,' laughed my father, who had joined us on a Zoom call.

'Still are!' My mother added with a smile.

I ignored that. 'Our blowout was over that hideous poncho, surely? Or was it fuelled by a surfeit of vegetables?'

I may love the produce of our Sherwood herb garden, our leafy lawn borders, and our bountiful vegetable patch, but I remembered a time when greens were an unwelcome addition to my meals. And hand-me-down clothing even more of an anathema. Especially oversized, out-of-fashion ponchos. I tried to recall how it had come into my possession but only had the vaguest of memories of a dusty cardboard box arriving with clothes allegedly 'from London', one late summer's day in Kolkata. Unexpectedly, it had my name on it, and because not many packages ever came for me, a grumpy, mostly ignored, newly-minted teen, I was at first unbelieving and then exceedingly excited. Ooh, I thought unpacking, what delights awaited me? I found soon enough that there weren't any. An aunt, looking to offload old clothes, had – out of the 'kindness of her heart' as her note told me – sent me a ton of hand-me-downs she claimed were haute couture.

Naturally, this occasioned some bristling. Which continued through our late-eighties North India trip a few months later. All the way till almost the end when things went kaboom. And that last time, it wasn't me exploding. I had just turned thirteen, and our holiday coincided with the onset of teenage troubles. Like bristling. And generational battles. And boys!

The bristling was over anything I was forced to do, and as any young person in an Indian family knows, that was most things. Food, fashion, friends, and family. Most of all, family. Oh, if you started counting the times you've had to bite back a retort or file away an interest or inclination because it didn't fit with the schemes of your family, it would number in the thousands. Having spent my formative years outside India, I had a pronounced individualistic streak that didn't sit well with the extended family, though my own parents were more flexible. This came roaring to the fore in my early teens, and because, very unfortunately, we always seemed to have relatives in tow back then, it meant the red-and-yellow poncho was not the only thing that clashed that holiday.

Over the next few years, the bristling on holiday was replaced, for the most part, with joy – not one of the many Bengali boys I knew of that name, but the feeling – as I became old enough to go where I wanted, and with whom I wanted. Travel became one of my greatest pleasures even when things went wrong, which they invariably did. But my sense of humour had taken over where the onerous uncles and aunts had left off, and I learnt to laugh off the turmoil. This plucky young woman I wanted to introduce to my children. But before that there was another, younger woman, an ugly duckling, made more hideous by a garish poncho, who was beginning to sense the direction in which she'd have to swim. To become a swan, if not a conventional swan.

So, as my father cleared his throat to tell my kids the tale of our 'Golden Veggie Triangle Trip', I dived in with my own account, pre-empting the inevitably inaccurate version of events that my parents would present. But as I waded into it determinedly, I could hear my parents' laughter on the steadily fading line as it disconnected of its own accord, checking out even before my story had begun.

4

Delhi and Rajasthan

The Golden Veggie Triangle

It did not start auspiciously when a traffic jam worse than usual on Howrah Bridge led to our abandoning our car, and with bag and baggage on head and in hand, we had to scurry across the gargantuan bridge, huffing and puffing and lamenting, to get to our train on time. 'We need to stop, my sari is unwinding!' complained my mother, who, despite having worn saris all her life, was prone to wardrobe malfunction. 'We will relax once we get on the Rajdhani,' said Baba doggedly, with emphasis on the word 'Rajdhani' as if that was all that was required to keep our travels from turning into travails, as they so often did.

The bridge was dirty, crowded, noisy, choked with fumes, and so very long that not only did hurrying across it feel like forever, but the bag and baggage we were lugging got heavier by the minute, tempting me to drop a few into the muddied Hooghly beneath. It was not as if anything in my suitcase of hand-me-downs was worth keeping! Certainly not the red-and-yellow poncho 'from London' I'd been made to pack against my will because it was a late autumn trip to 'chilly' (my parents were convinced) Rajasthan and Delhi. But I was thirteen and felt constantly in the wrong anyway, so I decided not to add to my long list of crimes by relieving myself of my luggage, trudging on behind my parents till we reached the train. In the nick of time too! It bridled with impatience as we got our worn-out suitcases and carcasses on, finding and settling down in our berths just as it let out a loud mechanical shriek to indicate it was leaving. People suddenly jumped up, as Indian crowds do, choosing that moment of utter chaos to stow away luggage, feed children, and crane out of windows. Then the train pulled away with a mighty tug and a whoosh. With the sun dipping, and our eyes drooping after our Herculean labours across Howrah Bridge, we fell asleep.

'How many do I have to bump off?'

'Just as many as always, I've told you before!'

'Not the little ones again? They're so cute!'

'Yes, them too. They get together and gang up on you if you don't get them first!'

It was still dark in the carriage, but I could hear these voices rumbling from near the window where, framed against the dawn, two large shadows hunched over a table, their faces close together. I half-opened an eye but stayed stock-still under the thin railway blanket. What villainy were they planning? They looked the part too; it became plain as the morning light trickled in. Big, bearded and hairy. With bandanas, and bulging, tattooed arms. And shades to prove how shady. Whispering in gravelly voices, from deep within their nefarious souls, they scanned the berths to ensure no one could hear them as they planned what must surely be a heist or mass murder.

I shrank farther back into mine to avoid being detected, because if they saw me, wouldn't they have to kill me? Knowing I was privy to their heinous plan? Just then the world was flooded with light, as if a curtain had been pulled away, exposing each player in that scene of terror. It turned out the dirty blue curtains that envelop each berth at night had indeed been pulled away, to reveal a relative standing in the aisle. The last relative I wanted to see, but the huddled men reacted even more adversely, looking up menacingly from the matters at hand which, I noticed for the first time, were chess pieces, rather than pawns in the terrible drama I was afraid they were hatching. They'd been peaceably playing chess, but now they turned their attention to the interloper: not tiny thirteen-year-old me, fortunately, but Tyara Mama, my squinty uncle.

How had we forgotten he was coming along on our Golden Triangle jaunt? If I had blocked out this horrible thought, there was no getting away from it now as he loomed over us, his lazy eye rolling from one inhabitant of our compartment to another. 'Chesh!' he bellowed. 'I was the college champion at chesh! Presidency College, no lesh!' Baba and Ma quickly called to the tea-seller in case a distraction could be devised, but neither the gangsters nor Tyara was to be denied their face-off. 'Nobody was spared my magnifishent moves!' he proclaimed. 'I was king! KING!'

'Really? Show us then, bruv,' said one of them so softly they might not have spoken at all. But for the first time Tyara seemed unsure. 'No, no, no,' he retracted, forcing an ingratiating smile. 'I don't want to spoil your game.'

'And how would you do that, bhai?' the bigger man with the beehive beard rumbled. 'Well,' spluttered our uncle, backing out into the aisle, 'I'd probably have the better moves.' Blanching as soon as he said it, realizing the trouble he was in, he made to run. Before he could, a big arm snaked out of the compartment to catch him. 'Oh,' averred the man with the arm (and quite possibly arms), his shades glimmering in the morning sunshine flooding the train, his mammoth shoulders nearly blotting it out, 'I don't think you want to see my moves.' And Tyara Mama ran, so hard, and so far apparently, that he must've reached Delhi before us because we didn't see him again till we got there.

Relatives were unavoidable on our childhood trips, as Baba avoided nice hotels at all cost. So stays with family and friends, no matter how uncomfortable, were de rigueur. From the station, we tootled over in an auto to the South Delhi home of an aunt with whom we'd been invited to stay, and were immediately entranced. Painted red and lost in a jungle of green, her house was even more fascinating inside, festooned as it was with art from floor to ceiling. My mother's cousin, an artist and Bohemian soul, with off-colour tales about the many men in her life, mostly artists like herself, often with peculiar peccadilloes, had the wonderful knack of quickly capturing those around her in pen and ink. Which she then presented with some ceremony. Like a large and exotic bird, she was extravagant in all that she did, providing entertainment to all, even the stallholders on the street below her balcony who would crane to watch whatever production she put on, by design or inadvertently.

As she'd made a series of our sketches, we gathered as instructed around her candlelit table, which filled the room with atmosphere and very little light. She had decked the table with what appeared to be exotic delicacies, including a large square tray in the middle filled with what we guessed was chocolate. But our aunt's performance was the main attraction, and the mystery of the dishes awaiting us was soon forgotten as she chanted and pirouetted around the room, waving peacock feather fans and long-handled paint brushes about in some sort of arty inauguration ceremony. We watched her with the same wonder and incomprehension as the bystanders below her window. It was all a great deal of fun.

After she'd rolled her eyes, and sung snatches of songs, she proceeded to hand the quite lovely pencil sketches over. Getting into the spirit of the thing, we bowed deeply as we received them, till she signalled the end of the proceedings with a wave of her kimonoed arms, 'And now eat!' Famished, we picked up our plates but were stumped with where to start, as we couldn't identify a single dish. This was when my six-year-old sister decided to take matters into her own hands, or nose as it happened. Sniffing at the tray of brown balls in the middle, she shouted out with the satisfaction of Archimedes in his bath, 'POO!'

In the pin-drop silence that ensued, with muffled scoldings from my parents, our aunt approached the tray with what appeared to be a horror equalling ours. But then, breathing it in deeply, she broke into one of her beatific smiles. 'Oh, YES, it is Kitty's litter! How on earth,' she giggled, 'did it get there?' As we attempted to think of reassuring things to say, she danced around the room some more and disappeared. For the night. After waiting a bit, we took ourselves off too. To an edible dinner and a plan for the morrow. Announcing with some trepidation the next morning that we were moving to another friend's place for the rest of the holiday, we were relieved when she appeared not to hear us at all. We left quietly, shutting the door behind us, as she painted away, oblivious to the world around her.

But no childhood holiday, no matter how humble, could be marred completely by the many maniacs that called themselves family. And Delhi had its attractions. If the Red Fort was splendidly theatrical, the drive through Chanakyapuri up to Rashtrapati Bhavan was wonderfully breezy, and we rolled down the windows to take in gulps of fresh air, along with the grand architecture. As we whizzed down one wide, elegant avenue after another, I was reminded of the freedom of my Manila years – the freedom to dream big, which I felt I had lost in the cramped and strict school of swots I was forced into on our return to Kolkata.

I dreamt big all the way to Delhi's shiny new sports and entertainment complex, the Asiad Village and American diner. Once again, I had a strong sense of déjà vu because a weekend ritual of ours in Manila had been bountiful ice cream sundaes on the beach. But here was something new. Something on top of the salivating that the anticipation of such ice cream brings. It was the tiniest tremor that started in my toes and sneaked to my tummy, wrapping itself around the hunger pangs and confusing me thoroughly. But it appeared to have sprung from the sight of not the ice cream tower headed my way, but the handsome waiter! Walking up to me in slow-mo like Pamela Anderson from *Baywatch* (but looking more like Matt Dillon), he bore the most gorgeous ice cream sundae, smothered in chopped nuts, whipped cream, brownie pieces and chocolate sauce. Then he opened his mouth and the spell was broken. 'Do you want aloo pakoras with this?' He had so misjudged me that not only did he lose his lustre, but the ice cream I was digging into diminished, too, before my eyes. Yet, a lesson had been learnt that day. Oh, not about books and covers, but that men bearing food would, forever after, have a magical hold on me.

But this epiphany did not overtake me till the very end of our Delhi sojourn. In the heat of the Dussehra blaze that consumed not just the Ravana effigy in C.R. Park, but the marquee, threatening to engulf the crowds as well, I was reminded of the cool of the diner, the sundae, and my bae-for-a-second. And in focusing on it, I was able to get through what had all the potential of becoming a tragedy. It started with the high spirits of all festival meets in India, with the 'para' (since it was C.R. Park; stronghold of domiciled Bengalis) gathering on the green around a brightly swathed marquee. They milled around the illuminations, dipping in and out of the marquee to pile their plates with food, the dazzle reflected in their finery. When the drummers started beating a steady tattoo, they converged at the grassy mound in the middle, where the lights sprang on to reveal the man of the moment – snarling, ten-headed Ravana himself, with arms outstretched to take on the world.

Was it any wonder his wrath knew no bounds once set ablaze, spilling over from his person to all that was around him? As the effigy burned, the flames licked the sky, rushing through the surrounding grass till it reached the wedding-cake marquee just beyond. At first, before anyone realized how big an inferno it had become, they continued to laugh and chatter, their faces aglow, their children dancing around, squealing happily. They were only alerted to the wild spread of the fire when a series of explosions emanated from somewhere near the marquee, and the children's squeals turned to fearful shrieks, with the adults lending voice. By then the marquee was undeniably ablaze, burning harder than the effigy, which had contorted and caramelized into a grotesque mass of heads, fangs, and fingers gripping weaponry. In its immediate vicinity, everything shimmered, collapsed, and was consumed.

'Bachao, bachao! Call the firemen, call the police!'

'Call the prime minister!'

'How did this happen?'

'What will the prime minister do?'

'Save the children!'

'And the food!'

'Babul tells me there were gas cylinders behind the marquee…'

'Will Babul tell the prime minister?'

'No, telling the firemen will do.'

The crowds retreated to the periphery once they had their children (and the odd plate of food) safe in their arms, to watch their festivities go up in smoke. Families with tired, despondent children began to wend their way home. We didn't see the fire engines arrive either, but we heard the next day that the conflagration was put out quickly in this well-heeled neighbourhood, away from the congested alleys and galis of Delhi.

~

The morning after we were on our way to Rajasthan in a cramped hired car. There was a nip in the air and I was wearing my red-and-yellow poncho again, smelling of smoke and jalebis, but without a tassel singed by the fire. Who knew that even hydra-headed, snarly-toothed Ravana would decline to touch the poncho, so monstrous was its appearance?

Hanuman was another matter altogether, and in fabled Chittor the poncho was snatched away. But we barely noticed till too late, so glorious was its ancient palace complex. Marvellously untouched, the graceful lines of the buildings stood sharply etched against the pink afternoon sky, as if the thousands of years of their existence had been the blink of an eye. With nothing cordoned off as they are nowadays, we wandered the corridors that lost civilizations had walked, drifted into rooms still humming with their voices, leaving those seductive whispers behind with reluctance when it was time to move on. I chose my own route through the palace rooms and courtyards, the temples and bathing squares. Occasionally emerging out of the cool shadows into the still hot sun, I could see the ubiquitous monkeys of North India, perched atop the spires and crenellations, silhouetted majestically against the sky. But as they bared their teeth to chatter in their usual devilish manner, any sense of quiet majesty was lost, and I retreated hurriedly into the cool embrace of the stone rooms again to dream of lost worlds.

In one such shadowy room, there was an unexplained shimmer at the far end. The flashes of light and colour were refractions not coming from any window. Easing up to it, my eyes dazzled, I realized it was a mirror – lonesome, in a dark, slumbering room, yet containing a world of revelations within. I knew as soon as I saw it (because I'd read my *Amar Chitra Katha*s even when abroad) that it was the fateful mirror of Rani Padmini. A mirror that can turn your life upside down, I pondered, peering into it with both trepidation and excitement. A topsy-turvy life seemed not a bad thing to a disaffected thirteen-year-old, but what I saw instead was a less awkward incarnation of myself. Undoubtedly because I wasn't wearing the poncho.

Feeling for the poncho, I realized it wasn't just missing in the mirror. I must have left it outside as I stepped into this smaller, stifling room, with its history-thick atmosphere pressing in. As the vision in the mirror faded, I spotted for the first time the monkey in the corner. It looked cute but odd, and for a fleeting second I thought that was because it was out of place in my fairy-tale mirror, till I realized its oddness came from the poncho it was wearing! Red and yellow went well with its long yellow teeth and laughing red face. Before I could react, however, the sartorially challenged (and yet looking better in it than I ever had) monkey scurried, followed by another handful I hadn't even spotted. Flying out of the room, as if on wings, like the monkeys from Oz, the first monkey was a red-and-yellow blur moving swiftly from temple top to palace roof, as I ran behind, miles behind, trying to get my poncho back. They were quick and far too clever, and it was beyond my reach in a trice. Left standing on the stone ground, I watched them disappear into the sunset, cold and, well, frankly relieved. Relieved of the poncho finally!

Of course with something so unmissable, my family was bound to notice it was gone, and mild recriminations followed. Yet, that was not the reason I regretted its loss, but that its absence made sustenance harder to come by for the rest of our trip. Throughout our whirlwind journey across Rajasthan, I had managed to eat well only because of my voluminous and too-ugly-to-scrutinize poncho. At most roadside eateries, as we rode in our hired car from vivid Jaipur to graceful Udaipur to magical-but-for-the-monkeys Chittor, the food on offer was purely vegetarian. The roti-dal-sabzi we consumed was filling and delicious, and I was happy enough to have it, till we got to the budget hotels that were our lot. These would have buffets laden with veggie delights, with a minuscule non-veg afterthought in the far corner. To those I gravitated after days of pure veg that had set my body grumbling, and with the help of my invisibility cloak, my so-ugly-it-blinds-you poncho, helped myself to the food I missed. Never more than a stray chicken leg, or a forgotten fillet of fish, I manoeuvred it past my sanctimonious uncle like the lost treasure of Sierra Madre, and savoured it as much.

But losing the poncho had its uses too. The teens are an age of certainty, where everything is black and white, and sticking to your guns of paramount importance. I had grown up in an unconventional, secular home, so the very idea of spending our holiday visiting shrines with our devout uncle was repugnant. No more for the need to wade barefoot into the litter of a hundred thousand pilgrims, which they felt necessary to lay at the feet of their gods before venturing into their sanctums, as the idea of obsequience to an omniscient imaginary being who played havoc with our lives. Struck by the serendipity of the loss of the poncho, which had doubled as a headdress in these places, I asked my uncle innocently, 'With nothing to cover my head, how can I go in?'

As Tyara Mama grumbled, my parents piped up unhelpfully with suggestions of shawls (which we didn't have), handkerchiefs (snotty), even paper napkins, nicked religiously at lunch in case of on-the-road emergencies, as replacement head coverings. The latter were in no hurry to rush into jam-packed places of worship either, but reluctant to offend family. I had no such scruples. At the next shrine in which my uncle insisted on wasting precious fortress-visiting time, I marched up to him with toilet paper draped over my head. 'I'm ready!' I beamed. While my parents admonished half-heartedly, my uncle chastised me for what felt like an eternity, rounding it off with the resounding, 'No more shrines for you, Madam!' If I had the poncho, I could have laughed into it and no one would've been the wiser, but as it was, I had to wait till I was safe in bed that night.

But if that was the end of pilgrimages, we hadn't seen the last of the hideous poncho; it became the recurring motif of my trip. I saw it disappear into the golden fortress of Jaisalmer, float past on the way to Udaipur Lake Palace, and at a truckstop for chai, I could have sworn I spotted it boiling in a pot. No one else in our party seemed to see it though, and I stopped mentioning it for fear of being dragged to a doctor. Till one day, they couldn't deny its omnipresence any more when it rode back into our lives on the shoulders of the most unlikely of carriers. Not, indeed, one of those mundane monkeys, but in Jaipur's jammed lanes of dusty pink houses and stalls of twinkling semi-precious stones, like early stars peeping out of the clouds, a dashing young American tourist walked up to us wearing it. The nerve, I breathed to myself, before I blushed and went mum.

Planting his booted feet in front of me like a movie cowboy, he chucked out his sculpted chin and looked into my eyes. As we stood facing off over the poncho, a million scenarios ran through my head. How had he got hold of it? Had the monkeys, dazzled by his blue eyes, offered it up to him? Had he, swinging from temple top to temple top like Indiana Jones, inveigled it away from them? For me? Like the Sultan and Rani Padmini? But how had he known it was mine, and managed to find me? Had he pursued me through Rajasthan to lay it at my feet? So many delicious questions. And years to discuss them surely.

But as I made ready to bat my dark lashes, I heard him say, 'Erm, can I pass please?' This confused me greatly, and I wondered if he wanted to do that Dirty Dancing thing. You know, where Patrick Swayze stands at one end of the room and Baby has to run its length to jump into his arms? All the better to heighten tension with. 'Excuse me,' he said again then, a trifle haughtier, 'let me past.'

'But,' I persisted, giving up on my romantic dreams even as I refused to give up on my possession, despised though it was, 'won't you return my poncho?'

'This?' he growled, pointing to the red-and-yellow vision dancing round his manly torso. 'This is MY poncho.' Taking a long, hard look at him then, I had to agree it suited his rosy-when-angry colouring better than mine. So I stepped aside, sighing a sigh that would reverberate through the years.

Pause for Thought: Travelling as a Twosome

'What did we even do on trips when we didn't have to manage the children?' I asked the husband, after a long, fun, but extremely tiring day out with the kids, involving lots of running about – much of it for fun, taking us to new places to try new experiences and learn new things. But some of it was just to ensure that things went to plan and the children were safe, warm, well-fed and moderately well-behaved. As well as engrossed!

Hence the question, as I flopped down on the sofa beside him after tucking the kids into bed. 'We must have had time to relax,' murmured Steve, drifting off now that he didn't have to keep his eyes permanently peeled on the sprogs. 'Are you sure?' I queried with amused scepticism. 'That's not how I remember them!'

'You don't even remember which trips were with me and which were with your former husband,' he teased gently, before checking out altogether. We'd had plans for the evening, though nothing more ambitious than a snack and TV. And if we were feeling especially limber, a cuddle on top. Nothing more taxing than that, but so bushed are we on holiday sometimes, after a full day with the tots, that even this can seem arduous.

As my partner of many years snoozed, I acknowledged the half-joking aspersion he'd cast on my memory; mine was a magical place that happily toyed with the past. So I took the opportunity to flick through the photos on my phone, like the many at home, in computer folders, even older paper folders, and tattered shoeboxes, to be dusted out to remind ourselves of our languid holidays of long-ago. 'Couples travel' certainly had its surfeit of serene, romantic moments, those golden opportunities that are now hard to snatch (but the intrepid parent still occasionally will, as we do). Yet, as bathed as they are in a rosy glow, grown hazy and more splendid with time and repeated reminisces, we do recall when nudged that there's been nearly as much chaos and hilarity in them as we've known with our kids.

That first holiday with your greatest love, if all goes well, will remain in your memory like a glowing orb. A golden haze of beautiful days that time cannot dim. Such was our first holiday together in the Wye Valley in Wales. This was followed by another romantic getaway to a log cabin in Derbyshire, England, for Christmas. Caught in a blizzard, we were snowed in for a week without sight or sound of another living soul till the New Year. But with a steamy jacuzzi and a large pantry full of succulent food, we made the best use of our time as a twosome, as only a loved-up young couple can.

Married the year after, our honeymoon took us to Corfu, an enchanted island in Greece, where we relished every moment from start to pregnant finish. Honeymoons can never go wrong, so deliriously in love are most newly-weds. The blips and bloopers on such a trip becoming mere flimflam to forget. Or so it would seem at the time. But find that shoebox of honeymoon snaps, and memories beyond the beauty of the setting, the sensuous days and nights, and the lovelight in your new spouse's eyes, will come flooding back. Especially the quirky, the funny, and the decidedly odd.

Because there's so much more to holidays as a twosome than romance. As time goes on and parental duties swamp, the spirit may remain willing, even the flesh might yearn, but other concerns take precedence. Over the years, our coupledom, on holiday and off, with children and without, has expanded into a camaraderie encompassing many shared passions. That's what makes the occasional couples' holiday for us now more than the marking of milestones (though that is often their apparent purpose), more even than the sum of their parts, but a celebration of a range of mutual, ever accruing, constantly deepening loves. And that sliver of delicious frisson that lives on in the twilight years. As well as the quirky, the funny, and the decidedly odd, which were there from the start, but only with the passing of time has one learnt to value them as much!

5

Corfu
Garden of the Gods

I had always wanted to go to Corfu. Ever since I was a child, devouring every last book about the Durrells and by the Durrells that I could find on the shelves of friends and family. And because being Bengali and middle-class established some amorphous connection with a posh but penniless, globetrotting English family, I found many, many volumes of their adventures in every home I haunted. They provided an escape into another world – more tranquil, but also more exciting, than my humdrum, hot and dusty existence in Kolkata. What made the Durrells' island paradise so magical for me as a child were the jewel-like colours with which they depicted it, the music in the voices they conveyed, and the rambunctious fun with which they infused every adventure. What a beautiful world! How I longed to be a part of it.

It remained an ember within me as I grew and struck out on my own, landing up in other locales that called my name. James Herriot's Yorkshire, for example. I started reading Herriot in my early teens because I found the characters endearing and the situations funny. 'In the streets, through the windows of the houses,' I read in *All Creatures Great and Small*, '...you could see the Fell rearing its calm, green bulk more than two thousand feet above the huddled roofs. There was a clarity in the air, a sense of space and airiness that made me feel I had shed something on the plain, twenty miles behind.' I didn't know then how deeply in love I would fall with the idyllic Yorkshire setting of Herriot's books. But ee by gum, a decade later I had moved lock, stock and hope-filled barrel to that part of the world. It had everything to do with the rolling green meadows, big blue skies, and bracing air in those veterinarian volumes, and much less with the marriage proposal I received from a son of that fertile soil, who got down on bended knee to become my first husband. I may have divorced him five years later, but I never fell out of love with Yorkshire. 'I could find other excuses to get out and sit on the crisp grass and look out over the airy roof of Yorkshire. It was like taking time out of life. Time to get things into perspective.' I regained perspective in those pea-green dales as well. I recognized it was time to move on.

After I married again, I found myself flying to Corfu at long last. And though the choice of destination for our honeymoon was decided on nothing more than a roll of the dice, there was a sense of inevitability about it. Of life taking control. So, from the start, this was a story of haunting as much as a honeymoon. Both together made it a tale of abiding love so great that it surprised me. I hadn't expected to love so intensely after the severe scarring from my first marriage, both literal and figurative. My first husband had turned violent within weeks of our wedding, and it had taken me more than four years to escape his clutches. But escape I did, to build a new life. To my amazement I loved again too, and more than ever before. It was easy because the man I hitched my star to this time was very different – with a fine mind and a big heart. That he looked good, cooked even better, and made me laugh, all proved persuasive as well.

When it came to picking a salubrious spot in which to honeymoon, we made like we wanted sun and sand and Ouzo like everyone else. We did indeed want to lap up the stifado (a gorgeous Greek lamb stew) with the Savatiano, whilst basking in the sun, but we had our own quixotic plans for the holiday. It would be a celebration of our love, but equally a celebration of everything else we loved: our shared passions. We planned to take the paths less travelled, landing up on rarely frequented beaches, supping on dishes that weren't tourists' fare, making our own delicious variations in the outdoor oven of our rented home. Besides walking through the olive groves, the deep green of the forests, and the barely tended fragrant orchards, to find half-ruined, maybe even abandoned, villas to admire. And to match them against what we knew of the Durrells' homesteads, to see if our discoveries weren't amongst them.

Yet, if our Greek island adventure remains with me to this day, if no other holiday has been as fruitful (in oh so many ways), it was not because it went to plan! If the greens and golds of Corfu beckoned, it was the dusty blue of my Indian passport that tripped us up before we even got there. Sending off my passport to their embassy in London, I hadn't imagined it would not come back stamped with permission to enter Greece. Wasn't it the most ancient and wise of cultures, the least prone to Johnny-come-lately European beliefs in white supremacy? But not only was my musty navy passport returned without the happily anticipated stamp, I was summoned to London too. After hours of queuing with other undesirables like myself, I was finally allowed in for an interview. My Greek interrogator looked as impervious as an Ionic column, till I started telling him about my lifelong interest in his country. And in the Durrells. At the mention of whom, his liquid eyes lit up; at my near-perfect recall of their adventures, his face relaxed into a smile; and with my vouchsafing of our intention to search Corfu's orchards and olive groves for their lost villas, he handed me the stamped passport with alacrity.

My ancient blue passport ran into trouble again at their even more ancient, ramshackle airport. 'What is this?' asked the sweating official, glaring at me, and then scrutinizing the document with narrowed eyes. Not entirely sure what he was questioning, I hazarded a guess, 'My passport?'

'I have never seen this before,' he huffed. I mulled this over and offered, 'That's because this is my first trip here.' To which he angrily exclaimed, holding my passport at arm's length as if it might explode, 'Never seen such a thing before!' Really mystified, I murmured, 'You've never seen a passport before?' Was it his first day on the job? At which he, and not my passport, exploded, 'Nobody has seen such a passport before! Where is it from?!' As I nervously shifted from foot to foot, never having come across such a thing either – an airport official who hadn't heard of India – and attempted to explain with gestures, shaping my hands into namastes, and worse, the Taj Mahal's onion domes, an older customs official took pity on me and came over to examine the offending item. I held my breath, expecting it to end badly, but then he grinned, 'Amitabh!' Yes, yes, I nodded, that's where I was from – the Land of Amitabh. 'I've met him once too,' I slipped in. 'Ooooo,' gushed the man, all excited, 'I loves Amitabhs, Missus Handles!' Fast-tracked out of the airport and into our tiny hired car, we were then released with smiles and waves into Corfu. All it had needed was our own Spiro.

Gasping on our drive to our rented villa, and not just because of the many hairpin bends in the hills we climbed, we scanned the melding of mountain and sea, one tumbling into another, yet standing out for their verve and beauty, with bated breath. Looking down from the hills as we rounded each bend, into the deep green of the olive groves in the valleys, we observed their brightening into golden green at the treetops, turning to azure as they touched the skies. The hills themselves were a patchwork of moss and sunlit green, chequered with yellow and orange orchards, and splashes of turquoise where the sea peeped through the gaps in the trees. Other shades shimmered where young farmworkers and older folk picking olives could be discerned, but for the most part, we saw no one at all.

Nearing the address I clutched in my hand, our surroundings grew shrouded, as the olive, lemon and cypress trees pressed in. A comforting embrace rather than an encroachment, the island held us closer still as we drove onto the last stretch of narrow track to our villa. The villa itself was dappled rather than dark. Some of it as deeply in the shade as the rest was gilded with light, as if it represented all of life in its balancing of dark and bright. If the approach was dimly soporific, and so were the cavernous rooms with their cool-to-the-feet tiles and sheets that enveloped like the sea, the glass doors at the back opened out to glorious sunshine and riotous colours. In its blossoming garden was a sunny patio and pool, around which we spent hours eating and reading, more often than swimming. Besides buying local produce at the colourful markets and delis we found, we also nicked the occasional lime, lemon or orange from the sunlit orchards beyond our holiday home. These went into our scrumptious alfresco meals, cooked with love, fresh air, and the occasional bug that fell in accidentally. So delicious were our days and nights, we could have just stayed put at our villa, but other passions beckoned.

Exploring the villages and beaches, we stopped to refuel at the open-air tavernas that dotted every jetty, roadside, and spit of white sand. As delicious as the food was, with an abundance of aubergine, lamb, and feta cheese, the joy of taverna-hopping was as much about the varying views it offered each time. The finest were, of course, on the beach, looking out at the cobalt blue Mediterranean Sea, but the roadside ones were perfect for watching people, who were as colourful and chaotic.

We enjoyed sniffing out markets just as much, some big and bustling, others secretively tucked away, and a few twinkling around harbours like seashells lost in the sand. From these we bought baskets of fresh, flavoursome food, and the occasional trinket. We swam in the sparkling sea too, but it was a cooler summer than usual, and more joy was to be had in walking along its pristine shore. These delights were entwined with our search for the Durrells' old villas – the strawberry pink, the daffodil yellow, and the snow white, preserved in my memory from childhood.

We decided to give many of the better-known and disputed sites a wide berth for the hidden gems, even if their links with that famous family were just as weak. This took us to many quiet lanes, overgrown copses, and deserted watering holes no one had set foot in in years. Some we set out to find and never did, some we discovered to be disappointing, so devoid were they of mystery and romance, and others we stumbled upon by chance. Many we drove up to, especially if they were on elevated ground, smelling of evergreens and dusk, so late in the day did we arrive after hours on the hunt. To get to a few though, we had to abandon the car and walk down dense tracks, following glimmers of sunlight, and our instinct for the hidden and the glorious. In an abandoned orchard we followed a pearly glow to find a diminutive but dazzling edifice that was well worth the nettle stings, but not likely to be the Durrells' snow-white villa for how few of their extensive menagerie of guests and pets it could have held. Down a path of long grasses heading out to sea, we discovered a vibrant yellow establishment, like a sunflower in a field. But we both agreed after a cursory search that it lacked the required je ne sais quoi to be their daffodil-yellow villa.

It was on our way back from this find that we decided to stop for a picnic in a sun-dappled olive grove we'd spied earlier. After a satisfying meal of fresh bread, olives (bought not picked!), and feta-stuffed tomatoes, we decided to explore. It was then that we discovered the house concealed in the cypress trees. A house we weren't expecting because it wasn't on our map. In a patch of land humming with life but deserted by humans, stood a faded ruby villa, large enough for a boisterous family and its many wards, but not so large that it couldn't lose itself with time and the onrush of vegetation. We circled it, standing on its vine-entwined porch, looking in through its weathered windows, but as desolate as it clearly was, it felt oddly lived-in too.

We sat on the porch, breathing in the tranquillity of the moment and the reticent beauty of our setting. When my husband put his arm around me, I lay my head on his shoulder, and a few kisses were exchanged. When he leaned in for the fifth (or thereabouts, I don't often count when kissing), we heard a noise in the house. It could have been a chair pulled back for a better look at what was outside. Or a harumph – the clearing of a human throat – to indicate the undetected presence of an onlooker. We jumped, casting around to ascertain who or what it could've been. 'Can you hear a goat?' my new husband hazarded, proving himself not very well acquainted with goats. I, on the other hand, had grown up in a part of Kolkata overrun with goats, and knew a cloven hooved critter when I heard one. 'Human, I think,'

I whispered to him, as we made for our car. We had largesse in the back, in the form of mouth-watering food with which we did not intend to part. Nor did we want to be arrested for trespassing, or for our spate of kisses. Scrambling into the car, we were sure it felt more crowded than when we drove in, yet thought nothing further of it.

Suddenly our serene villa was quiet no longer. We heard the tread of unfamiliar footsteps in the empty kitchen. The splash of water when no one was in the pool. Whispers in the garden that weren't leaves in the breeze. And on one occasion, another of those harumphs we'd heard at the apparently abandoned villa. Most of all, we were overtaken by a strong sense of being watched, though not in a lascivious way, despite the feeling that some of this observation followed us into the bedroom. It seemed as dispassionate but well intentioned as a naturalist studying his subjects. I almost expected to hear David Attenborough's well-known voice, with that relaxed but knowledgeable commentary that grace all his engrossing programmes, but this time holding forth on *us*, and our youthful and amorous activities. That was when it dawned on me who it had to be – Gerry Durrell! Who else could be so amiably interested in animal activity? Who would be haunting his old strawberry pink villa, which we'd stumbled upon just days ago, but him? And hadn't we felt like we'd been followed home from there? Who could it be but the patron saint of travellers to Corfu?

In the end, whether we found the Durrells' villas in Corfu or not, we found something else for sure. Something more exciting. When we returned to Nottingham, the first stirrings started. Great waves of morning sickness assailed me for weeks till I took the tests that told us we were undoubtedly in the 'My Family and Other Animals' way. Exploring Corfu that languorous summer's week with my second husband, I had not only discovered that it was every bit as full of life as Gerald had promised, but that this life was catching. When our baby boy came along eight months later, we did not call him Gerry. Nor was his little sister, joining us eighteen months after, called Geri. But bizarrely, as soon as they could talk, that was what both of them independently decided to name their first teddies.

6

Amsterdam

Sex, Drugs, and Sunflowers

The colours of this Amsterdam evening are jewel-like. Everything has a fluidity, a swirly-whirliness, like daubs on an Impressionist's canvas. I seem to have found my way into a Van Gogh painting.

But my mind refuses to pin this perplexing idea down long enough to find out how. It skitters from thought to half-baked thought till it returns to the unsettling world around me. There are women behind panes of glass, bathed in a red light bleeding into the sidewalks. The pavements shift beneath my feet, threatening to come up and meet me.

I am walking through Amsterdam high, high as a kite. Though it has made me acutely aware of every fibre of my being, and every atom of the world around me, I feel disconnected from *people*. My husband of many years, father of my children and best friend, is walking beside me, but he feels miles away. We look at each other with the startled surprise of strangers who find themselves in an embarrassingly intimate situation. With a dazed grin, he confides that the pavement is bucking 'like a bronco'. Giving him my 'You seem nice but I'm married' smile, I hurry past, only to backtrack as I recall I'm married to *him*.

How did we get here?

After a half-decade of loving, responsible parenting, we decided that we desperately needed a grown-up bacchanalian bender. We picked Amsterdam for that purpose, convinced that at nearly forty, with kids, careers and other clutter, this would be our last hurrah. To make it a dirty weekend to remember, we had solicited hints and debauched tips.

'Gotta have 'em hash brownies,' said a friend.

'Must hang out at a Proeflokaal,' said another, urging us to visit the city's famed gin joints.

'Try a threesome with a prostitute,' suggested one, as we goggled. 'You only pay half-price for the second person.'

Despite our best intentions to be hard-nosed hedonists, we are gripped on arrival by an overwhelming urge to simply stroll hand-in-hand through the picturesque network of canals that is more quintessentially Amsterdam than any of its other delights. We stroll past a stunted skyline of narrow houses with stepped or bell-shaped roofs, each with a pulley and hook at the top to allow furniture to be hauled directly to the upper floors, circumventing narrow stairways. The mesh of bridges takes us past flocks of brightly coloured houseboats (often patriotically orange) and pretty little boutiques, delis, and cafés from which we accumulated hats, clogs, cheese and cups of bitterballen (not-bitter-at-all meatballs).

We find little gems like Begijnhof, a walled square where pious spinsters once sought sanctuary. It is quiet and historic but we are reminded that we're in the most liberal of cities when we spot a roof-front statue of The Virgin in an advanced state of déshabillé. Rambling through the flower market, ablaze with tulips and tourists despite the foul weather, we arrive at Rembrandthuis with its jolly red-and-green shuttered windows, where we disappointingly learn that the genius was also a jerk.

In the evening, the city is a brightly lit cosmopolis despite its intimate feel. We chat with believers in the pagoda at Chinatown and wash down hunks of steak with Gancia at one of the many Argentinian steakhouses. But the time is ripe for a spot of debauchery, so we take a walk on the wild side.

The Red Light District is a surreal place – not depraved or degenerate, just otherworldly. A lurid crimson light bathes everything. Animated neon people display amazing sexual agility, while flashing signs promise over-the-top adventures. 'Live sex,' one screams. 'Anything goes,' assures another. The hundreds of sex shops are as giggle-inducing as they are bewildering. Hoping to bag a curiosity, we end up so puzzled with what was meant to go where that we leave empty-handed (but with a gaggle to Google). Before that though, we spot a must-have item for the adventurous lady: a bicycle with male equipment attached to its seat, so she arrives at every destination, satisfied.

While the crowd gawks and giggles, stray groups of men stride past with a sense of purpose, some in fancy dress. There are Vikings, knights and, appropriately for how hesitantly they approach their targets, chickens. But the lure of the place is the women in their illuminated windows, unabashedly displaying their wares in a manner that's uniquely Amsterdam. Gingerly stepping past body parts thrust at us, we stop to catch our breath, only to find a window-woman beckoning. We nudge each other, grinning sheepishly. She holds up three fingers to indicate she'd have us both. But getting only gauche laughter in response, she marches out to fix us with an exasperated glare. 'Are you coming in?' she asks. 'I am counting to five!' What could the cloistered parents of two toddlers do but scamper? We run like we haven't in years, breathless, laughing, all the way to our plush hotel where, after aeons, we catch up on coitus without interruptus.

On a roll now, our next stop is the best little hash house in town, 'Baba's'. (Who knew my dad had such an interesting sideline?) We inch into its hashish haze to the strains of a sitar and the smell of incense, watched by the giant Ganesh in the corner. Bolting down our massive chocolate slabs of wooziness, we head for our long-anticipated Indonesian dinner.

If any experience could be stranger than walking through Amsterdam on a high, dining out in the same condition must be it. We sit there teetering as the world around us reels and jigs. The waiter takes orders in an extra loud but sympathetic voice. (Stoned customers? All in a day's work.) Steaming dish after delicious exotic dish arrives and is wolfed down hungrily even as I try to ignore the riveted gaze of the man a few tables down. Had my sex appeal grown exponentially in the last hour, or am I making a spectacular mess of the meal?

Our bizarrely enhanced hearing also makes us unwilling eavesdroppers on the seduction at the next table. A grizzled elderly man is schmoozing his way into a night of geriatric passion with a blue-rinsed old dear.

'Sex, you see,' he says, 'is not for the young.'

'No,' she rolls her eyes at us. 'They don't appreciate the nuances, the delicacy…'

That we are the young of their conversation pleases us no end, and Hubby suddenly snaps out of his trance to suggest we attempt 'the nuances'. But even as I try to tell him that I am in no state to know where things should go, my chair starts keeling over, and the lights blink crazily. I rush out to breathe in fresh air and sanity. Behind me, I hear running footsteps, and then there's darkness.

I wake to sunshine and stability. Gently propping me up, Hubby asks if I am up to a bit of Van Gogh.

The Van Gogh museum is being refurbished, so we head out to where the cream of the collection is being housed: The Hermitage. A square, spare building with the brilliance of Van Gogh on every wall, it is the perfect place to commune with the artist on his birth anniversary. As we wander among the paintings, breathing in every brush stroke, every vivid shade and inspired choice of subject, we find what we have come to Amsterdam for: a high more genuine than the sex emporia or hash houses can provide. On Van Gogh's canvases is a passion that lifts us like nothing other than our beautiful children can.

Linking hands, we whisper and smile. We gaze reverently at the sublime *Sunflowers*, *Irises*, and *The Yellow House*. Then stopping to scrutinize that most famous of nightscapes at the end of the hall, *The Café Terrace at Night*, we are more than a little surprised when, with a great whoosh, we are sucked into it.

Pause for Thought: Going Solo

'You don't really know who you are till you've travelled on your own,' I decided to tell the children one day. In the old playroom now converted to a family library, we were each immersed in our own pursuits. While our daughter was sitting in the light flooding through the bay window deftly modelling a scene from Shakespeare's *The Tempest* from plasticine, the son was strumming absently on his guitar in the big armchair in the shadows. He was playing the Harry Potter theme tune. I sat on the chequered rug in the sun, beside our snoozing dog, tinkering on my laptop with my column that month, whilst holding forth on the joys of solo travel.

'But you like travelling with us, don't you?' our young lady of ten asked. 'Of course!' I beamed. 'I *prefer* journeys with you, because nowadays I find that even when travelling on my own, I am thinking of you because you are not with me, and not spending my time following my fancies as I would have imagined. But there was a time, at a younger age, when I enjoyed it far more. It taught me a great deal, especially about myself.'

'What did you find out? Did you discover how goofy you were?' the young man, now twelve, teased from the depths of the velvety orange armchair, going back to twanging on his guitar, where he had seamlessly moved on to Lou Reed's

'Perfect Day'. Pulling a face at him, I confirmed, 'That's exactly what I found out, and you know what? That is really important to know. Travelling solo, where there are few external pushes and pulls, is a great opportunity to learn about yourself. It also tells you who you are in a crisis. This important knowledge you can then carry into your everyday life to ease your passage through the world.'

'Now you sound like my form teacher! Or *Vogue* and *Cosmopolitan*,' our daughter chuckled, as she put the finishing touches on an ethereal Ariel.

'Or a guidebook for the lone traveller, especially when female. Find your inner goddess! Do yoga! Try Tao Chi! What about mud baths?' I joined in the laughter. 'But no, I don't mean that kind of prescribed and fashionable solo tripping at all. I mean doing your own thing, on your own once in a while, or at stages in your life when you're seeking a better understanding of your surroundings, and yourself.'

Self-help books and advice columns do indeed insist you discover the wonders of you, and many advocate travel as the means to do that. Where, in the midst of exploring the world around you, you also uncover the one inside you. There is a lot of truth in that but many of the instructions that go with it are hooey, I said to my children (including the dog who had her ears pricked as if listening to my sage advice), as I counted on my fingers the proscriptions you must never follow. And a couple that you should.

Don't buy every guidebook you find, do your own research instead. Watch a film set in your destination, talk to people who have visited. Make an itinerary by all means, but don't feel you have to stick to it if you're drawn to something else. Ensure it's about following *your* heart and passions. Don't feel you have to measure up to anyone else, least of all, idealized travellers in magazines or on the internet. Be adventurous, but don't feel you have to do things that aren't for you just because they're 'cool'. Don't bungee jump if it doesn't appeal. And if you'd rather retire early than go clubbing, to watch the stars from your window, that's just what you should do! Equally, if there's something you've always fancied, but never had the courage to try, on your own in an exciting new place is a good time.

Most of all, go with the flow. An unfamiliar spot will present opportunities to savour life that you wouldn't even have thought of. The best things happen when you leave it a little to chance. It is in those moments of serendipity and unexpected delight that you find yourself. And even the courage for a new life.

7

Zurich
Moo-ving On

To the strains of the church organ playing quietly on a sun-drenched late afternoon, splashes of colour coalesce on the mosaicked floor; they dart, spin, and fuse into a shimmering pool. Then they fling themselves apart to become solitary spots again. Preparing for sundown, the sun dips behind the quintet of stained glass windows before which I sit entranced, and the dance of the techni-coloured sunbeams take on a new urgency. Inside the darkening church, Zurich's famous Fraumünster, I am as rapt in this waltz of the elements as I am mesmerized by the magnificence of the windows I have wandered in to see. Panes of such breathtaking beauty created by the artist Marc Chagall in the seventies, that it draws thousands to this ninth-century Swiss church annually. Today, its dazzling dance with the sun, and the rare semi-deserted state of the church, lured me in, even though I hadn't come to see it. I hadn't even known it was here – these windows, that church, or this cobbled street. Or that I would find such peace in it. I hadn't planned any of it!

In fact, I hadn't even planned on being in Zurich. After four years of putting one foot in front of the other to get from one day to the next, of meticulously planning and executing survival strategies to keep, not just going, but alive, all I wanted was to *be*. I had been in a violent marriage for too long. One that had left me battered and bewildered. To make matters worse, I had been serving out this time in a strange city far from the one I called home. The northern English city of Sheffield and Kolkata, my hometown, were 5,000 miles and much else apart. Yet, ironically, the tonic I required was the same anonymity: of a city that didn't know me, to lose myself in, and shed the skin I was about to outgrow. And to learn quickly, like only a new place will allow, to revel in the weightlessness of being without it.

But lucre-loving, sharp-suited Zurich, the jewel, or indeed bank vault of Switzerland, wasn't the sort of place people went to for spiritual healing, was it? Doesn't enlightenment blossom where souls, rather than bank balances, grow? Did Buddha find any greenbacks under the Bodhgaya tree? No, he found nirvana. And yet, much has been mended amidst the mountains and lakes of Switzerland. From Heidi's wheelchair-bound friend finding her feet, to the dawning awareness of Thomas Mann's magical mountain-dwellers, to the well-heeled Victorian hordes who convalesced from consumption, catatonia, and conjunctivitis in Swiss (and swish) sanatoriums – history is studded with stories of the Alps conferring a kind of peace. So, when circumstance and the generosity of a friend put me in this unexpected place that late summer sixteen years ago, I partook of this peace too. A piece of chocolate to be precise. And cheese. And a great, big wedge of good cheer.

I started walking that first crisply sunny morning, without plan, purpose or destination in mind. And I found, on top of the delicious by-products of cows with which I'd begun my day (soft cheese on fresh bread with a steaming mug of hot chocolate), cows themselves. Cows by the dairy truckload. Cows of an unusual persuasion. Not the divine bovines or gau-matas of Hindutva, but quarts more fun.

Ambling past the deep blue of Lake Zurich, where families read, ate and basked in the sun, and couples canoodled on brightly bobbing boats, I came upon a flamboyant bottleneck of people and stalls. Hagglers and happy browsers had descended on a flea market full of antique wares where the roads narrowed and became cobbled. But I pushed ahead to older things still. Just beyond it loomed Old Zurich Town, a self-contained world of elegant mansions, grand münsters, and quaint yet fashionable shops and restaurants. I couldn't wait to nose around, discover its sophisticated delights, yet round the corner and up a hill, and my nose had led me straight to a cow. Muddy, musty, hefty cows with consternation in their eyes I had encountered plenty before, both in England and in India. But a vivid orange, gold, and eggshell blue cow? A life-sized, hand-painted, pipe-smoking cow? I did a double take.

It really was gripping an oversized pipe in its shiny, oversized teeth. I looked around me for a tobacconist's to explain its presence. Or a chocolatier or cheesemonger's at least? But in the absence of any, it had to be a charming anomaly. I chuckled and walked on, feeling decidedly lighter. Like one of the sandbags holding me down had shifted.

Three houses down, while admiring their well-maintained facades, I was brought up short again. I had spotted another cow. A pretty pink one wearing a bonnet, looking down from one of the many wrought-iron balconies that adorn Zurich apartments, especially in this old quarter. A large cow was an improbable thing to have on a tiny veranda but there it was. As I tittered at the tight fit and even more ludicrous headdress, further weight lifted off my heart.

But taking the next turn gave me another turn. I was looking into the eyes, no, eye, of a pirate cow with a sequinned eyepatch and the jolliest red bandana. As I reached out and touched the first one I'd dared to, my fingers left quick-fading prints on its now patently obvious fibreglass body. And this time, there really was a lovely little chocolatier's nestling behind it, with every conceivable cocoa-infused confection on its shelves. It twinkled with fairy lights and smelt of heaven. At the behest of the bubbly lady behind the counter, I sampled and I swigged. I then took my purchases to a tiny table outside, and scoffed half of everything I'd bought to the strains of a most accomplished roadside orchestra. My husband might have sneered, 'Cow!', yet, all of a sudden, it had the ring of a compliment, and another wound had scabbed over.

I meandered through more winding streets then, full of stalls selling fresh produce, a jaunty parade that seemed to spring from nowhere, and a charcuterie from which billowed mouth-wateringly meaty smoke. Smiling back at the young man who'd twinkled at me from behind its bar, I resolved to return for lunch the next day. Admiration felt lovely after so long, but I was now on a mission more important than snagging a man. I had cows to spot. And this time, I wanted to understand them too: What were these bovine beauties about? Who made them and why were they here?

The day had begun to shorten, and a slight wind picked up as I made my way down a series of stone steps to the Fraumünster on Münsterhof. And lo and behold, another classy, glassy duo came into sight just then. These were perfectly turned out in pastels, as if in their Sunday best, with their placid snouts pointing churchwards, and beside them for the first time, a placard! These ubercool cows fashioned from fibreglass were, I learnt, the work of the sculptor Pascal Knapp, commissioned by the Swiss tourism board to add points of interest to the already beguiling Altstadt. Yet, they had done so much more! As the lowering sun lit up the gorgeous Chagall windows of the Fraumünster, I was drawn into its stately stone interiors, now dappled with dancing light. Settling into a pew, I thought about the unexpected delights of my unplanned holiday. With every en-cow-nter, I had lost something. The dread that had lived with me for so many years. The shackles that had bound me for as many. But with every sighting, I had gained something too. The pounds from all the chocolate and cheese wolfed in the vicinity of these cows of course, but also the giggles, the wonder at their very existence, and the confidence that I had all the joie de vivre required to see myself through a nasty divorce and out the other side. Every utterly-butterly bovine friend I'd made had not only sent me into peals of laughter (which drew human smiles in return), but a little bit closer to tranquillity, and battle-readiness.

Because if you do not seek, you'll most likely find. I did.

8

Sheffield
Nerves of Steel

'In this town of Sheffield…
The streets are narrow and the houses dark and black.'
– DANIEL DEFOE

I arrived as an accidental settler in Sheffield in the new
millennium. Swept up in a typically impetuous romance
with an Englishman on holiday, I ended up leaving everything
behind to marry him. It was to be a shiny new adventure in
a brand new place – new continent, country, and city. But
Sheffield in 2000 was moribund with that moss-damp smell
and underfoot-squelch of a cemetery after the rains. With
the same graveyard stillness. I awoke to a town trapped in a
time-warp, mourning its destruction in World War II and
the demise of its busy steel industry; every bit the city of

The Full Monty, but with a thick, black vein of deep despair I was unprepared for.

And my exciting adventure? It died young. Our romance lasted as long as we toured England, with the Jaguar S-TYPE purring through banks of hedgerow, down narrow country lanes, under yew tree and oak, with birds chirruping on every branch. The greenness of the landscape, the creaminess of the clotted cream that crowned our wayside scones, and the glow cast by this little island's long list of literary lights whose legacy was simply everywhere – everything I fell in love with while exploring England died a death in Sheffield.

It was green but forever obscured by grey sheets of rain. The clotted cream was no less creamy but with a bitter aftertaste as my marriage went sour. And violent, as my new husband turned out to have the pugilistic predilection of every disaffected man in the gritty, low-cost northern English films I'd watched. But while there was no joy to be found in my deteriorating domestic situation, I detected a hint of magic in Sheffield. I would have to bring it to the fore, like others before me...

The ancient heart of South Yorkshire, Sheffield began as a settlement in a forest clearing beside the River Sheaf in the first millennium AD. Post-conquest, the normans built Sheffield Castle to tighten their grip on the north and a small town mushroomed around it. By 1600, its prodigious output of top-notch cutlery had transformed it into a boom-town. But the English Civil War saw widespread death and destruction in Sheffield, including the demolition of its castle in 1648. Its fortunes revived temporarily with large-scale steel production in the eighteenth century, but these factories, when drafted to make World War II weapons, nearly brought about the city's annihilation from German bomb raids. The sixteen successive attacks of 1940 flattened the city and killed many. To this day, the trauma of the Sheffield Blitz weighs heavily on its soul, with mournful discussions on it at pubs and 'greasy spoons'. But death, having got its hooks into this city, hasn't left since. The long, thin smokestacks — the remains of its steelworks — resemble the spindly legs of skeletons against its granite sky. The decrepit concrete towers at the heart of the city look shuttered and forbidding. The dingy train station, subterranean pedestrian walks and dank car parks add to the Dickensian air of decay.

I soon realized I was morphing into Sheffield, but that wasn't all bad: swaddled shabbily against the marauding cold, frumpy and unadorned, but with a steely resolve to find my way out of my nightmare. And so I went looking for the hidden delights of my new home. I found beautiful churches in winding lanes. I learnt to enjoy working man's cider at the haunted Queen's Head, the oldest pub in Sheffield. I salivated my way through a whole street of cosmopolitan grub. On Wednesdays, I spent my last pound on a falafel at the Lebanese deli, and on Thursdays, I gazed hungrily at the display in the patisserie. I wandered around a spider's web of cobbled streets behind venerable Sheffield Cathedral, and in secret squares I discovered pretty little shops snoozing in the timorous sunshine.

In Orchard Square, a woman who made exquisite jewellery watched as I sketched a funky bangle for her. Did I want a job as her designer she asked, mostly serious. No, I said regretfully, I work nine to five, and when I get home … well, when I get home, stuff happens. Come back, she said, if circumstances change.

The central Tudor Square became my refuge at noon. Flanked by the cultural trinity of Sheffield, the Lyceum and Crucible theatres, and the grand art deco Central Library, it's a sunshine trap but also the core of all that's cultured in this down-at-heel city. This is where the annual World Snooker Championships are held, from where they were to be snatched and transplanted to a posh southern conurbation, but Sheffield held on. This is where I ate my baguette every day (and sometimes my falafel). It was three-storeyed Waterstones though, crammed to the rafters with books, which became my best friend.

Then one day, I knew I had the confidence and enough start-a-new-life funds to make my escape from my husband – and Sheffield. That afternoon I found myself outside a stately Victorian house, a solicitor's office I'd seen in passing while exploring the cobbled lanes. Through the divorce as my husband raged, I read in the attic room with a chair wedged against the door. My life was about to change.

And so was Sheffield's. The city had just signed up for a new regeneration programme that would transform this tatty town into a shiny, vital entity again. I wanted vibrant for myself too, and was ready to leave the setting of the worst years of my life. Sheffield began building, buffing, and polishing just as I upped sticks. But there were loose ends to tie that kept bringing me back, and each time there was more revitalization bustle and more marvels to behold. The Winter Garden, the largest urban glasshouse in Europe, with more than 2,000 plants from around the world, opened in 2003, becoming the first beautiful thing to blossom in Sheffield in a while. Springing up alongside was the Millennium Gallery, a glass palace for the city's finest art.

Three years later, a vast, gleaming new train station with a 263-foot art deco water feature had risen from the ashes of the old to much fanfare. The original had opened under very different circumstances in 1870 on a cold, damp, cheerless Sheffield day. Over time, a combination of wartime bombing and flooding by the River Sheaf, which flows underneath, caused damage so irreparable that millions were required to restore the station. But it was this transformation that changed Sheffield's fortunes. The rest of England started streaming through its doors.

The city then set to work on its squat concrete skyline. As part of an ambitious plan to reclaim its beautiful historic buildings, they began gutting and replacing the innards of once-glorious Carmel House while restoring its grand old facade to former glory. The unapologetic demolition of the worst of the concrete monstrosities from the sixties followed. Before I left Sheffield forever, I witnessed the terrifyingly ugly 'Egg Box', the marriage registry office in which I'd said yes one fateful day, bite the dust. I was not the only one cheering.

My own return to vivacity proceeded apace with Sheffield's. I bought a home in Nottingham and then, eventually, met and married the love of my life.

Today, I am back in Sheffield, at a trendy bistro in the heart of town. As I wait for my best friend to appear, I think of the marvellous turn my life has taken. I reflect on my beautiful toddlers and their amazing father. I think about the many writing assignments streaming in, including this one. I look around me and see the stunner that is Sheffield now and feel no bitterness. It has the air of a fashionable European city. There are well-dressed Yuppies hogging the best tables at the chic cafés dotting this central square. There are sparkling new hotels and a colourful continental food fair on the focal green where Sheffield's human detritus once slopped about. There is sunshine and laughter and happiness. I breathe in this new city.

This time, it smells good.

9

Nottingham

Second Chances in Sherwood

When I moved from industrial Sheffield to leafy Nottingham, the legendary town of my childhood books about Robin Hood, I was ecstatic. I would have blue skies, green trees, and birdsong instead of chimney stacks. My new husband and I had bought a sunlit red-brick house with a timeless air. And walnut trees, a moss-topped pond, and barely tended orchards behind. With it, the promise of living our own Robin Hood romance.

A few summers on, I found myself in the last stages of a pregnancy that had rendered me so vast that nothing other than reading and dreaming in the shade of our walnut grove was possible. The intervening years had been packed with weddings and work. But here, at last, was the chance to revisit Robin's world. In our creaky wooden swing by the centuries-old wall that separates our garden from the wilderness beyond, I read of his return from the Crusades to find himself stripped of title and estate. Forced to take refuge in Sherwood Forest, not many miles from our home, he forged a band of outlaws into a fighting unit that could counter the might of the dastardly Sheriff of Nottingham. I decided to visit the many fascinating spots connected with Robin the moment my little bundle arrived.

But Blighty locales linked to Robin are legion, because he wasn't just one man. History is full of men coming out of nowhere to lead armies of ordinary folk against their oppressors. The Robin we know is a masterful amalgamation of them all. Thousands of years apart, he surfaced in places as distant as Berkshire in the south and York in the north. Yorkshire has strong claims to this most enduring of English heroes. But the earliest ballads, dating back to the fifteenth century, place him firmly in Sherwood Forest in Nottingham, and it is here we now feel his spirited presence.

Sherwood Forest once covered most of Middle England; today, it's just over a thousand acres, but still serenely beautiful. Deep in these woods stands the Major Oak. Legend has it that Robin hid from the Sheriff's men in the inlets of this 1000-year-old tree. The summer we went looking for it, with not one but two toddlers, we found it down a dappled walk flanked by towering trees. It looked every bit the elder statesman – its leafy green mane nodding gently in the sun, its potentate-stout trunk deeply gnarled with age. Intrigued by the elaborate scaffolding encircling it and the mysterious recesses that Robin must have used to elude his enemies, the toddlers disappeared down an egress like the White Rabbit. Squeezing my much-reduced form into an opening, I followed their giggles to find my little wood sprites comfortably ensconced in a hollow. Before Robin could draft them into his merry band, I lured them out with the promise of a scrumptious picnic.

Smoked salmon and cream cheese sandwiches washed down with ginger beer later, we strolled to charming Edwinstowe in whose twelfth-century church Robin had married valiant Maid Marian. The pretty Norman church of St Mary's had a shuttered look that bright summer's day, as if shielding its glorious past from the marauding sun. Swinging the heavy wooden door open, we wandered down the aisle like Marian and Robin, sat in the pews to imbibe the otherworldly atmosphere, and lit a candle to their enduring love as we left.

Stopping on the way home for aromatic cheese, chunky steaks, and fresh strawberries from the busy farmers' market in Old Market Square, we were reminded that Robin is omnipresent in Nottingham. Next to the square are the Galleries of Justice from which Robin escaped the Sheriff's noose for the umpteenth time. On the brooding hill overlooking it is Nottingham Castle, once the Sheriff's fortified residence. The squat Victorian museum built on the ruins of the demolished castle has retained that watchful air. More excitingly, alongside the continuing municipal role of the Sheriff of Nottingham, there is now an 'official' Robin Hood, who will show you round his city, in familiar forest-green gear.

Robin lived dangerously, loved intensely, and died in style. He is reputed to have breathed his last at nearby Newstead Abbey, long before the dashing Lord Byron took it over.

Wounded, he was put in the care of its nuns, who poisoned him. But not till he'd shot one last signature arrow into the forest, warning his Merry Men of impending doom. This story is also ascribed to Kirklees Priory in Yorkshire, but Newstead's eerie splendour compels you to believe.

Today, Nottingham is imbued with Robin's indomitable spirit. Our patch of Sherwood bursts with life and colour after every winter chill. My children grow like flowering ivy towards the sun. From my perch on our ancient wall, I see them chase butterflies and tumble over hedges. I watch with concern and then relief as they pick themselves up, laughing off little bumps and grazes. I pick up my pen and start writing. 'Like Robin, I have travelled from the East, to this place of beauty, love, and second chances.'

Pause for Thought: Qualities of a Tripfella

A lot of the time it's your companions that make your holiday. The perfect setting, season, mindset, time of life, and even budget may not be enough to save a holiday if you don't have the perfect companion. And by perfect, I mean perfect for you because there is no gold standard, and don't let anyone tell you different.

For one traveller, their tripfella's ability to navigate new cities might be essential, or their predilection for risks. For others, it might be their composure in the face of catastrophe that matters, or how good they are at selfies. Whilst for some of us, it is good nature that clinches it, alongside an open mind, manifest in the ability to immerse themselves in the good times while providing support in the bad.

What you need is a mental checklist of the most important qualities you require in your tripmate. As in life and romance, it's crucial to have the right companion on trips too. Get it right and they enhance enjoyment, but get it wrong and your holiday goes down the pan. If it is your life partner you are trippin' with and you're still in the full bloom of love, you can't go wrong. But if it isn't someone that close, or conversely, *so* close that familiarity has bred contempt and the situation begun to stifle, then proceed with caution.

Make yourself a hot cuppa, wrap up in a warm, fluffy blanket, then plonk yourself down in your favourite seat. Comfortable? Well, that's how comfortable you need to be with your travel companion, or it'll never work. Then, like a tot's schoolwork where you match pictures with words, consider if the companion you have in mind fits with your holiday setting, the season, and your philosophy of life and travel. Are they at ease with one or more?

If they are with some, but not others, weigh up which of these you most treasure; do they value them as much? If they love Italy, which is where you're heading, and want to explore and absorb as much as you do, but are allergic to springtime pollen, for example, you may want to reschedule. But if they are happy whatever the weather, yet can't abide the Greeks or their architecture, when it's a trip to *Greece* you're planning, it's your trip-buddy you may want to reconsider. No one ticks enough boxes, you say? Well, go on your own, my friend. A solo sojourn is infinitely better than one with the wrong tripfella. Even the most eagerly awaited break can become a nightmare in conditions (or with people) with which you're at odds. But, if by some miracle, they fulfil every prerequisite, ticking every box – if they have a sense of humour, a sense of wonder, and just plain good sense – don't leave home without them! Ever!

Just occasionally, however, conflict and disarray can make a holiday momentous. It can certainly make you respond to situations differently, and take you down unlikely paths. Most of all, it can open your eyes. About the person with you, or yourself, or both. It can tell you a powerful truth about your life. And lead you to change it forever.

10

New York and Las Vegas
Lady Liberty

Stopped and frisked at every possible opportunity from Heathrow to Newark in New York, I was getting heartily sick of it. Especially as the same treatment wasn't being meted out to my then-husband, George, a white Englishman. He was smilingly ushered through every checkpoint, whilst I was scowled at suspiciously, batted to and fro like a shuttlecock, and searched within an inch of molestation. To add injury to insult, I was rugby tackled, or should I say American footballed, as we walked towards the exit, because I hadn't realized I was meant to stay back for further indignities, while my husband was allowed to walk freely into the 'Land of Liberty'.

This rough reception was not entirely unexpected. A year before we set out on our Yankee adventure, the Twin Towers had come down in the blink of a bewildered eye, when a plane had been flown into the first tower, as if by accident. But then

76

a second followed, by no means an accident, and changed our world forever. The horror that ensued is indelibly imprinted in our minds twenty years on, so it was not surprising that the summer after was fraught with fear and suspicion for Americans, and retribution and restrictions for the rest of us. Especially 'brown people', which the alleged perpetrators were, although regular brown people all over the world shared America's sorrow. Relatively safe from America's ire in Britain, we knew I'd face travel restrictions, suspicion, and harassment if I were to wander their way. Yet, explore the seething cauldron of conflict that was the United States, on a lacklustre budget, was just what the then-husband insisted on doing that very summer.

After the humiliation I had endured at the hands of the American authorities for a mere single-entry tourist visa, which included their demand for a letter from my husband vouching for my good intent, topped by the mistreatment I suffered in transit, I was ready for a relaxing holiday. Our Jamaican taxi driver, however, had other ideas, speeding all the way from the airport to our hotel on Broadway. He had reason to be angry with his world because America had not been treating his kind (or mine) very well, but it rebounded on *us* that morning as he dumped us with our baggage a few blocks from our hotel. It was becoming steadily clear that conflict would be at the core of our trip. But it would also be memorable and funny, despite everything.

More nonplussed tourist faces greeted us on Broadway than even at the airport, but it was not till we drew closer to the object of their attention that we realized why. They had just set eyes on a Broadway regular – the Naked Cowboy. On an island illuminated by the bright lights of the city was a man with long blonde hair and a six-gallon hat. His well-dressed head was the antithesis of everything below, where all he had to cover his crown jewels was a guitar. Try as we might, we could not keep our eyes from straying to his … er, guitar, so we hurried on to rather more essential, and hopefully, restful things. Our hotel.

Restful turned out to be the wrong description for it. The hotel receptionist was hostile, and the accommodation, despite being at the heart of Broadway and flanked by glittering theatres on every side, unwelcoming. My already plummeting heart sank to my toes when I saw the poky room we'd been given, discovering not long after the broken lights and contrary toilet. Its clatter and roar made our little room shake and, I was afraid, the corridor as well. Where were the sunny smiles and shiny vistas of their movies and TV shows? Sorely disappointed and bone tired, I fell asleep.

When I woke deep in the night and looked out the room's lone window, an unexpectedly large window, I saw the lights still blazing on Broadway. Even at that hour, I could see customers in cafés and diners, and in the darker lanes winding away from the hub, revellers returning home in the timorous light of the impending dawn, as the headlights of vans making early deliveries swept over the first of the joggers taking advantage of a quietly contemplative city. Truly the city that never sleeps, I thought, and warmed to it.

The morning found us in another yellow cab, but a friendly one, taking us to 'Sex' (the first 'e' and 's' having fittingly dropped off Essex) Street for breakfast at Katz's, the world-famous Jewish deli. From small beginnings in 1888, Katz's had become an NYC institution, feeding flavoursome pastrami, fluffy matzo balls and hearty latkes to folks like Al Gore, Johnny Depp, and Bruce Willis. At the counter, fast-talking bakers helped us choose from the briskets, bagels, knishes, knoblewursts, and more, on display. Settling down with our feathery pastry and lightly spiced meat in a sunlit seat, we watched the city begin its hustle. A colourful collection of ethnicities gathered at the bus stop. The neighbourhood patriarchs were setting up shop, putting out fresh produce under stripy awnings that shielded from the burning New York sun. But it was early and still cool.

Inside, a man expertly sliced and arranged salami under glass. Listening to the bustle of the bakers kneading, twisting, and tossing dough, I was transported to the world of eighties' romcoms, big hair, and food so good it was positively orgasmic. When Harry met Sally here in 1989, Meg Ryan pulled off the most famous fake orgasm in cinematic history. It's clear why they picked Katz's for that sensual, yet funny, scene. Neither swish, nor shiny, it oozes character. As I looked around with interest, a dapper older man appeared at my shoulder with my longed-for iced tea. He flashed the toothiest of American smiles when I asked him about that Meg Ryan moment.

'She wasn't faking it, you know,' he confided, 'it was the best she ever had.' Adding, as he walked away, 'You're sitting exactly where she sat that day!'

I shot to the other end of the seat. I didn't want to wallow in Meg's afterglow, but I was totally taken with the idea that not only was she not faking, she'd never had better. And that my toothy friend had been *instrumental*. I looked around to find him amused still. I smiled in response, as my husband whose presence I'd nearly forgotten after yet another row, glowered at us both.

Then it was George's turn to choose a destination, and so began a day of eyeballing all the usual suspects, starting with the Statue of Liberty. After gawping at it from the ferry because that year, after 9/11, tourists were barred from historic Staten Island on which it stands, we decided to lunch at Catherine Zeta Jones's favourite bistro on what turned out to be the worst omelette ever (true of almost everything we ate in New York), wrapping it up with a chase down the block by the maître d' who wanted a bigger tip than we could afford.

That lack of lucre also meant we walked everywhere that week. Walking through the blistering barrios, with thoughts of a break on a shady park bench, till we discovered just how shady when we found it bristling with used hypodermic needles, we arrived at Ground Zero. Or all that remained of the bombed and gutted Twin Towers, at the root of much of my troubles in the US, and a smouldering symbol of so much that was tragic and wrong with the world. The word 'root' described it perfectly too because that vast wound in the ground looked so much like an uprooted forest, or the aftermath of a root canal on a giant's aching jaws.

We kept walking, and though there was no plan to visit movie locations, everywhere we went had been one.

From Wall Street, where I expected Michael Douglas's Gordon Gekko to slither past us, as we craned at the faux-roman buildings and big, brassy statues, to the humongous toy store FAO Schwarz from the film *Big*, in which the dazzling show of plenty seemed less about childhood joy than adult greed. As dusk was falling, we arrived at the Empire State Building, with the glittering spread of New York beneath it. Suddenly the weary feet, the crass commercialism of almost everything we'd seen, including the giant King Kongs in the giftshop near the top, ceased to matter, because up there in the stars, looking down on the twinkling city, was the American dream at last. On our last day in New York, strolling to the piers through an almost European street with its cobbles and cafés, I saw beauty by day too. Having argued with my husband (again), I ran ahead and stood looking out at the shimmering sea, the sailboats sharply etched against a clear blue sky, and knew there were infinite possibilities still waiting for me. I was only twenty-eight.

Flying to Las Vegas on a cramped American flight where the passengers were too large for their seats, and the turbulence from the thunder and lightning unsettling (on another trip I might have deemed it dramatic), I found both the hotel room and the food considerably better than in New York, but the company just as bad. At the MGM Hotel's Star Trek Experience, embarrassed by George's discourtesy to a Klingon on Captain Picard's Bridge, I asked to be let out mid-event. My 'Beam me up, Scotty!' muttered unconvincingly, but with an ingratiating smile, drew glares from the Trekkies, but unexpectedly did the trick.

My greatest joy became breakfast at the hotel. Like everything else in Las Vegas, breakfast was larger than life: mile-long buffet tables tottering under the weight of enormous pancakes oozing sticky-sweet maple syrup, steaming tureens of scrambled eggs, and still-sizzling bacon stacked high on seductively large plates. You could pile your plate high as many times as you pleased. Not just the food, but everything was large, flashy, overflowing, and not for me at all, but I decided to approach it with humour and a social anthropologist's interest in alien life.

Touring the many grand casinos felt as much like entering an alternate reality as it did sightseeing. Jiggling to each on streetcars with singing drivers, we sometimes spotted an Elvis impersonator, and sometimes a showgirl strolling languidly to work, her tail feathers aquiver. Without much money, gambling was not the pull of our vague Vegas wanderings, but the wealth of sights and sounds at the casinos. The lure of lucre brought in poseurs you could spend all day watching, but there were other wonders waiting, equally faux. Venetia with its delicious gelato and gondoliers, and a marvellous manufactured sky I would have happily gazed at for hours had I not been moved on by the same officious American type whose job it was to harass non-whites. The pirate ship extravaganza at The Mirage, with music, dance and cannonballs firing to mark each glitzy Las Vegas evening was genuinely entertaining. As were the card sharps, conmen, and pop-eyed tourists, all circling each other like sharks in the giant tanks of Mandalay Bay Resort & Casino.

On the afternoon we were leaving Las Vegas, we decided to splurge a little, having our last American meal at Bellagio of *Ocean's Eleven* fame. The tough venison and the tougher waitress were not worth the money we spent, nor even the plush corridors we padded through, or the swanky casino halls we peeped into (all we could do with no dosh left to spend). But then we sauntered out of the casino to its picturesque palm-lined drive, and in a flash it was all made worthwhile. As I scanned its sky-high fountains brushing the bluest of skies, with the lofty Vegas skyline behind, I sensed something in the offing. Something momentous. The jets of water gracefully glided back and forth to popular tunes, till Andrea Bocelli and Sarah Brightman struck the first notes to Andrew Lloyd Webber's 'Time to Say Goodbye', at which they ceased being fountains and became the surge of feelings deep within my soul. Feelings I'd kept submerged broke free and soared with the dancing spray. As the song reached its crescendo, piercing the languid afternoon and the soporific Nevada air swaddling me, I woke from the years-long sleep I'd spiralled into.

It was indeed time to say goodbye. To Las Vegas and America. Neither of which was a hardship. But to my marriage too, which was a bigger leap to take, though it had been a nightmare throughout. Like the fountain jets that winched those great waves of water, the weight of that failed relationship had finally begun to lift, and though it would take another four years of strategizing and squirrelling funds, that swansong on a hot American afternoon marked the start, for me, of a return to vitality.

Pause for Thought: Stop and Smell the Kaapi

Sometimes the place is less important than the pace. Or all that you pack your trip full of. Because it isn't only your luggage you pack; you take with you your plans and intentions, strategies, wisdom, dreams, and desires. Sometimes the place can pale in comparison to what you manage to do there. Or in not managing to do very much, the peace you find.

Another essential to pack for a trip is the right companion. Someone with whom you lurrvve having fun, but equally, a bud, a mate, a chum with whom you're happy doing nothing at all. Because sometimes you don't want to pack your trip with very much at all. Sometimes what you *don't* feel compelled to do is as important. It's often that which sets a holiday apart from daily life, if yours is as frenetic as ours. Full of children, pets, their schools and recreational activities, the house and its garden, and our full-time jobs. Then there are parents and siblings and friends. Not to mention doctors, plumbers, taxmen and more. The upkeep of it all can be exhausting. If you can then get away occasionally to tranquillity and indolence, it is a break in the real sense of the word.

Being able to do that is an art however; hard to achieve but an absolute delight when you get it right. Because pleasurable indolence is never a vacuum, filled as it is with love and

84

laughter, slow and easy sensual joys, and rest – delicious, much-needed recuperation. But it can be tough to attain in the treadmill of our lives (except suddenly in lockdown we are pedalling back, taking our foot off the gas, and that may be the best thing to come out of it).

With the ideal travel companion, it is indeed possible to have a perfectly glorious time doing very little, and it speaks volumes for how well you might gel in life. Because life isn't always exciting, but with that attuned partner, it can be contented a lot of the time. That's how I discovered that the man with whom I was spending oodles of splendid time, on trips and off, after my disastrous first marriage, made not just the perfect tripfella, but life partner as well. Our trips together sealed the deal, because you're guaranteed to see past a tripfella's facade amidst the stresses and strains of the unfamiliar surroundings and unexpected situations that travel brings. You also get a measure of how deeply they enjoy life. My second husband knew how to drink life to the lees, even as he capably handled every on-trip crisis. What I didn't know was that he couldn't unwind. No more than me!

Neither of us was good at relaxing, though we didn't fill our holidays with extreme sports or any other laudable activity. But we did keep busy, imbibing all we could. Of course, we knew we shouldn't rush from one experience to the next. We knew we should stop and smell the roses, and in fact, we did. But we also smelled the coffee in the morning, the coffee liqueur at the end of the night, and everything in between. If one of us had half a mind to relax, the other suddenly became a whirlwind of activity carrying us both along. As if slowing down might mean squandering an opportunity to learn, to see and feel. But with barely a moment's pause on our satisfyingly exhausting everydays *as well as* holidays, we'd begun to broach the idea of that much-needed lazy, languorous, barely-out-of-bed break. We wouldn't just smell the kaapi, but slowwwly breathe it in.

11

Odisha and Kerala
Southern Comfort

With my second husband, I took it slow before I said 'I do'. More because it felt right rather than it didn't; because the feeling right I wasn't used to. So we'd been together several years, though married only a few months, and heavily pregnant too, when we decided to undertake a trip to Kerala to 'relax'.

Leading up to it had been busy, even frenetic, with not a moment to rest. We'd moved houses. Both giving up smaller houses in two different British cities to buy a family home together in Nottingham. Once settled into our new home, a red-brick haven in a walnut copse, we had tons of fun planning and even more, celebrating, our wedding at Charles Darwin's sprawling old stone home in the rolling greens of Derbyshire.

From which the next stage of our lives together evolved. I discovered I was pregnant with our first baby.

Our Kerala holiday had been arranged months before our life-changing discovery. We had been looking forward to sunshine and houseboats and seafood. With news of our first pregnancy, we knew there would be sacrifices to make, of our beloved seafood for example, but had no clue exactly how much would have to change; so we planned an exciting itinerary anyway. An itinerary that did involve lots of sun, and a houseboat, and plenty of exploring as well.

We had learnt some useful lessons from a similar holiday in Odisha a few years before that. We knew better than to book ourselves into decrepit old hotels, as romantic as they might sound. We knew not to expect perfect, or even predictable, weather, as rain followed us wherever we went. And we knew to keep only half-an-ear open to the rumblings of distant connections in India, eagerly warning us of the mosquito menace. Distant maashis were once again making dire predictions, this time about the dangers of holidaying whilst pregnant. They warned us against a bewildering array of infections, foods, transport that moved more than an inch at a time, and everything else besides! Amongst the vast range of terrible ailments I might catch and pass on to Baby was the hitherto-unheard-of chikungunya. Sounding more like a roadside snack than a dreaded disease, we nevertheless looked it up and decided to proceed with our trip. Cautiously. But Kerala looked so wholesome: all water, sunshine, and fried fish. What could go wrong?

Flying into Kochi with the intention of spending a day exploring it, before moving on to the backwaters, we started out in the cool of the morning. We sauntered along the picturesque seafront, stopping to gaze at the famous Chinese nets, and the hustle and bustle on the docks around them. Seeking some quiet, we wandered into the Church of St Francis, famous for its connection to the circumnavigator of the globe, Vasco da Gama. This old church with its bare, chalky pink walls and defunct punkahs was testament to his having lived, loved, and worshipped in Kochi. Sitting in a pew, waiting for our feet to stop aching, we wished the punkahs were working as the sun was near its zenith. We couldn't leave Kochi without visiting its famous bazaars however, so we headed into the sunshine again.

Not far from the church were lanes full of shops of crafts and spices, delighting both the artist in me and the chef in my new husband. Breathing in the colours and fragrances of these streets, we found ourselves in the most famous one – Jew Street. Once the beating heart of the Jewish community, it was now a maze of antiques and spice stalls, both indigenous and exotic, a wonderland of flavours and scents into which we waded happily. Till it started getting the better of me. Not only did the smells overwhelm like they would any pregnant woman, but the sunshine and blindingly white buildings baking in the sun dazzled a tad too much. Telling myself this hectic day's travel would be offset by the rest of our trip, where we'd do nothing but relax, we wound up our explorations to head off into the blue yonder, or Kerala's famed backwaters, where a cottage on stilts, beside a heron-thronged lake, awaited. It would be pure bliss.

We had found just such a cottage in Puri two years before, on a pristine beach, but not before we'd been forced to run from the ghouls and geckos of the haunted colonial hotel we had booked ourselves into, on the recommendations of friends who were perhaps less sensitive to things that crept and those that crawled. In fact, I had visited that hotel as a child and retained wonderful memories, but when I returned on a bright summer's day, everything about that hotel had belied the light and cheer around it. A cold gloom enveloped us as we walked in to a disinterested receptionist handing out keys. Or key, as we appeared to be the only guests there. The room we were shown to was darker still and the furniture festooned with cobwebs, attempting to brush which aside, I managed to disgorge an avalanche of creepy crawlies on me, including a very large lizard!

Nearly phobic about lizards, this was the last straw, and grabbing my lover's hand, I ran out the door and up the driveway, oblivious to the enraged shouts of the hotel management behind me. I didn't know why they were chasing us as they already had our money, but fortunately not our luggage, which my partner had picked up as we ran pell-mell out the hotel. At the top of the drive, a serendipitous getaway awaited us, in the form of a rickshaw driver taking a long drag of something. But he reacted with alacrity when we asked him to make haste, carrying us away on his chariot as if he'd been waiting to do that all his life. Before we knew it, we were settled into a much nicer hotel – serene and stylish with a lovely sea view.

Yet, little could beat the view from where we stayed in Kerala. Our cottage on stilts, to which we strolled on collecting our keys, was deep in the forest, with a ladder to our bedroom and a balcony around it for torchlight chats and alfresco meals. Plus, a hammock from which to watch the sun go down. From our bamboo balcony, we could also see backwater birds of every hue, hear fish splashing and frogs croaking, and spy the twinkle of houseboats. We had plans to drift slowly on one of those, into a delicious stupor. But till then, there was a restaurant by the water, also on stilts, in which to eat ambient meals. The food was strangely always North Indian, as were the customers – most of whom were jewellery-jangling honeymooners. But after lunch, there was our hammock on the lagoon to retire to for the afternoon, away from their cacophony, with ice cream delivered to our door. And as the sun dipped, so could we, in the infinity pool stretching out to sea. It was shaping nicely into the languid holiday we had promised ourselves.

It was also strongly reminiscent of our idyllic afternoons in Puri, lounging in the cottage balcony, in between forays into the kidney-shaped hotel pool which it overlooked. Outside the garden in which our cottages clustered, was the hotel's quiet beach, in whose white sands crawled tiny ruby-red crabs, vendors with colourful wares, sand sculptors building worlds on shifting sands, and nightie-clad 'aunties' who frowned upon us frolicking in the sea, though unlike them, we were fully clothed. Every time I ventured into the sea to splash harmlessly, albeit with a white man, legions of aunties appeared out of nowhere to glare, forcing our retreat to our cottage where, fortunately, we had much to occupy us. Including puzzling over the perkiness of the erotic sculptures dotted around the hotel. Were they spared the wilting gaze of the aunties?

But even if decadence is not a precondition of being western, what they say about mad dogs and Englishmen is perfectly true. They can't sit still. They must explore. And conquer. And so, we set out two days after we'd arrived in Kerala to explore the backwaters, but on foot. It would be an amble, the husband said. A brisk fifteen-minute trot round the lagoon was the perfect exercise for pregnant women, he stated with a straight face. We'd be back in our hammock eating ice cream before I even knew it, he reassured. So we went on our 'little stroll' to see more of our salubrious surroundings.

At first our explorations were interesting, but as the day wore on and my pregnancy weighed heavily on me, I huffed and puffed and flagged. My feet dragged, and my throat felt parched. With the sun at its height, a slow burn of reluctance and resentment overtook me too as we pushed on past the hotel grounds to the sleepy hamlets beyond. Looking over at my husband, who'd been full of beans, I could see he had begun to look a trifle sapped as well in the scorching heat, and pinker than was healthy for him. 'Shall we head back?' we asked simultaneously, and agreed with infinite relief.

Never again, I told myself on the interminable walk back, would I try that whilst pregnant. Worrying about Baby in fact kept me up that night. It was then that I heard the intruder in our room. The previous two nights, I had half-heard the rustling, but dismissed it in my sleep as part of my dream, or Steve. But now, wide awake and sitting up inside the mosquito net, I could see it wasn't him. Although emanating from outside the net, it was definitely in our room, which was pitch black. I recalled that I'd noticed items disturbed in our room before, but hadn't been sure it wasn't the work of hotel maintenance. There was definitely someone rummaging through things now, and maintenance didn't usually happen at this time of night!

Frozen to begin with, I knew I had to act when the rustling and scratching grew. But should I tangle with the trespasser myself, or wake my still peacefully sleeping husband? What if there was more than one intruder? Even as I prevaricated, my husband, awakened by the mounting scrunching and squeaking, tiptoed out of the net to switch the light on. We saw our night-time intruder for the first time, with relief and a smidgeon of disgust. It was a very, and I mean VERY, large lizard. Contemplatively munching on the banana on the dressing table, it did not seem to care that we'd spotted it. Only stopping to look at us briefly, it went back to the banana with no intention of leaving our room. Happy to share our bananas with it but not our room, we decided to lure our unwanted guest out by flinging the remaining banana out the balcony door. Deciding that bananas were always greener on the other side, our large lizard lumbered off after it, followed by the resounding slam of our shutting door. In the morning, as if nothing had happened, there were only herons to be seen on the balcony. But in my very pregnant, peace-craving condition, I was glad to be moving to the houseboat that afternoon.

How striking the houseboat looked against the blue sky and sun as we boarded, with the gorgeous green of Kerala's backwaters lapping against its sides. The boat itself was intricately crafted with graceful bamboo arcs and fine lattice. As the captain and his mate ushered us in, I daydreamed about the languid couple of days we would spend on it. But the daydream dispersed like ripples from a distant boat, as we looked around ours. My excited heart started to sink, deep into the heavy waters of the lagoon on which we floated. Deep, deep down to the sandy bottom. Not only was the houseboat terribly shabby, it even seemed dirty, and for some reason, the larger bedroom was occupied by a group of men who claimed to be crew. We hadn't seen them when boarding, just the captain's sunny smile; and stumbling upon them sitting sullenly in the dark bedroom gave me quite a turn. Did we need a staff of twelve, I wondered, and felt uneasy. Worse, they appeared to have bagged the only clean and comfortable bedroom. Scanning the dingy bedroom reserved for us, I suspected I would not last the night.

But out on the covered deck with armchairs, chilled nimbu pani, and a beautiful view, I was lulled into forgetting. Gliding over the backwaters, with its captain at its helm casting a lazy eye over our blue-green vista, the boat made such gentle progress that perched or swimming water birds barely batted an eye. Our cares took wing instead.

As evening descended however, the darkness and heat pressed closer. That we were on a cramped boat, and unable to walk off, began to dawn on me. But worse was to come. First, the mosquitoes arrived in droves, and with them, the dread of chikungunya that the maashis had drilled into me. It was, I had been told, particularly perilous in pregnancy. Then came the legions of lizards, and after our recent run-in with one, I felt unprepared for more. The thought of bugs and reptiles swarming over us as we slept in the houseboat's claustrophobic bedroom was too much for me. And as the beautiful view from the deck had been snuffed out like a candle by the setting sun, my attempt to stick it out gave way to my maternal instinct shrilly telling me to get off that boat.

But what choice did we have, having given up our cottage in the backwaters, and not due in Kochi till the next day? A little shiver sailed down my spine when I realized to what extent we were at the mercy of our shady houseboat crew. Fortunately, the husband had read fewer Robert Louis Stevenson books, and convinced me I could persuade the crew to help us off the boat and into comfortable lodgings on terra firma. I found myself telling them our baby was due, which, heavily pregnant and panicking as I was, was almost true. In the wink of a pirate's eye, our menace of sailors morphed into clucking matrons, carefully helping us off the boat and on the road to Kochi (it helped that we'd paid in full already).

'You'll be fine, Madam, not to worry.'

'Aiyo, all will be well. I foresee healthy baby!'

'We will do the needful. We are like this wonly!'

When I expressed concern about the 'needful', they assured us they would take us to the city. Though at that time of night, and in the back of beyond, it would have to be a long trek on foot. And so it was that we marched through dusty villages with the head boatman leading the way with a kerosene lamp and stout walking stick, like a scene from Richard Attenborough's *Gandhi*. Without film spotlights to guide us through the pitch dark though, we could barely see where we were going. But the boatmen sang as they marched, and though it didn't ease our passage, it kept us entertained. Even the baby jigged now and then, till we came to the city. The hustle and bustle of even a quiet town like Kochi hit us like a refreshing waft of wind after the darkness and silence of the backwater hamlets. 'What kind of hotel do you want, Madam?' asked the head boatman. One without creepy crawlies, I thought but said instead, 'Comfortable for my "condition", please.' He took a good, hard look at my ready-to-pop pregnant tummy and delivered us to the Taj. In a comfortably cool room overlooking the sea that night, after a delicious meal of Kerala style fish, I finally got some sleep.

The swish of water had lulled us to sleep every night in Puri too, but the watery gusts engulfing us at the top of a Konark temple was quite another matter. Another of those unexpected adventures we so regularly got swept up in on holiday, there wasn't even a whiff of one as we made our way to that ancient complex of sandstone temples. Sprawling and stately, Konark was also preternaturally quiet that morning, like nothing in India ever is these days. We might have stepped back in time, so hushed was our ascent up the wide stone steps to the platforms where exquisitely carved lovers embraced. As our wonder turned to titters every now and then, so realistically did the statues writhe, we tore our eyes from them to the green tops of the trees, and down to the bazaar at the gates where the usual hubbub hadn't begun yet.

This tranquil time-travel bubble was rudely burst, however, when the trickle of tourists turned into a flood. They spotted us and decided, as happens bewilderingly often in India, that my white partner was in fact a celebrity. Someone worth getting to know at any rate. Nearly shoving me aside to throng around Steve, they pressed him with questions.

'You come from foreign?'

'Maybe Bilet?'

'You know that old woman with the hats? The Queen?'

'So cute! You are that Prince Hari, no?'

Despite his protestations, it ended the way it always did: with a flurry of handshakes and chits of paper thrust at him, blank ones for his autograph, and phone numbers they wanted him to keep.

That storm of attention was just the start of a stream of disturbances. Unlike the crowds that had cosied up to us, the weather turned progressively unfriendly, and then dangerous. Having climbed in the sunshine to the highest and most exposed part, to get a panoramic view of the fabled complex (and escape Steve's 'fans'), we hadn't noticed the gathering clouds. When the rain began to fall, soon whipped into a frenzy by the wind, we were too high up to make our way down safely, so we hid behind a ledge. Under a gaggle of acrobatic stone lovers who'd made us giggle just moments before. But now, buffeted by the howling wind and blinded by the rain, we were no longer laughing.

As the wind hurled itself at us and the rain lashed, we clung to the erotica and each other, entreating it to stop. In the end, with no sign of it letting up, we made a rain-blinded scramble to the bottom. To shelter under a more capacious ledge, a less erotic threesome, for an eternity before it was safe to strike out in search of our hired car. Heading back to the hotel, we saw whole roads and villages underwater, and a trail of fallen trees. 'Ma'am,' they exclaimed, when we walked back into our hotel lobby, sopping wet, with twigs and leaves stuck to our hair, and mud caking our shoes, 'please don't leave the hotel today. Odisha has been hit by a cyclone!' Thanking them profusely for their timely intervention, we took to our bed for the day, hiding under the covers with hot cups of ginger–cardamom tea and pakoras till the morning after. Which we spent, in fact that whole day, watching the majesty of the stormy sea. But from a safe distance.

We did get our relaxed holiday after all, on each occasion, but not before becoming embroiled in the turbulence we seem to inevitably attract.

12

Manila
Call of the Sea

I think I have always loved the sea. Born in Kolkata, the pearl perched on the Bay of Bengal, we were never far from it. Yet, as my hometown was a river port, it wasn't an amble away either. I have no memory of beaches from my early years, though we would have undoubtedly done the Bengali thing of visiting Digha and Puri to splash ankle-deep in the sea, before settling down to enormous seafood dinners. But in the long months of the Kolkata monsoons, I imagined I could smell the sea in the driving rain. Till the waters rose on the roads, drowning that fresh sea smell in the odour of flotsam and filthy jetsam. But Bengalis, especially those born in East Bengal, which my father was, do have an affinity to the sea, not just for its fruit in shorsher jhol, but a kinship more elemental.

So, when his job took us to the Philippines, a knot of islands in the Pacific, for the most formative part of my childhood, we all slipped into a new way of life with reasonable ease. My father and mother emerged from their shells to become social butterflies, gaining a reputation for their ramp walking, Rabindrasangeet and gulab jamuns. My younger sister was the ultimate party animal, lying in wait for aunts and uncles at shindigs, especially uncles, to sit on their laps and warble songs, dressed in frilly spaghetti-string frocks. She was a toddler at the time, so there was no suggestion that it might become a problem in later life (to be fair, it did not). The social whirl of our lives in Manila, however, did not suit me, but then I did find my niche, and it was by the sea, or at least near any window from which you could see and breathe it in. With the sea breeze ruffling my shapeless preteen hair, I could happily read, draw, and dream for hours.

Moving to the Philippines was not just a change of setting, it was like going forward in time. Eighties' Manila under the Marcos regime was very keen on its cosmetic appeal, and a world away from the Kolkata of the seventies I'd grown up in. Makati, where we settled, was a wealthy area of gated neighbourhoods. Full of bankers, diplomats, and a large international community, it had swept all its troubles to the poorer margins of the city, and was spick and span and beautiful. Under an almost perpetually blue sky, the buildings sparkled whitely, the shopping malls were full of shiny gizmos I'd never seen before, and everything sprawled – schools and parks and homes.

Houses in this area often came with palm-fringed private pools and a retinue of servants. Ours didn't, but was a lovely split-level house with more outdoor space than I had in Kolkata. It was only towards the end of our Manila years that I discovered that all of the Philippines didn't live like that, but in cramped homes, often cheek by jowl with tragedy. But one saw none of this in swish Makati, in which we lived for half a decade. Till, with the overthrow of the Marcos regime and the onset of a violent tussle between factions, we returned to India, suddenly aware that our fate from start to finish had been in the hands of two people addicted to solid gold taps, shiny shoes, and widespread murder.

India in the seventies and eighties was a shuttered society, gazing inwardly as it kept global influences out. This left it a little down-in-the-mouth as well as down-at-heel. A little like how Hollywood has always depicted Soviet Russia – so purposeful it lacked pizzazz. But I was a child, and sparkle mattered, and it just so happened that we had arrived at the height of the Philippines' shiniest epoch, superficial though it turned out to be, and the contrast with a then-shabbier India was a jolt. What captured my heart was not the shiny malls, or the big houses and pools, not even the fancy clothes and toys not yet available in India, but the freedom. I loved having little supervision.

I wandered these islands, where the weather was almost always fine (with cyclones and earthquakes appearing like summer lightning to disappear just as quickly), the streets clean and wide, and the beaches pristinely sandy, on my little blue bicycle. I took books with me wherever I went, and bubblegum, which inevitably got caught in my hair but never in the way of my reading. Unlike in India, where there were always adults questioning your every move, whether they knew you or not, nobody took any interest in Manila. Back then, this was bliss (though, as a mother now I find it problematic). Nor was there anyone stopping me from wearing shorts, or humming what pop song I wanted, Madonna's 'Like a Virgin' for example, which I didn't have to fully understand to know it would be frowned upon in Ballygunge Phari.

I was invisible like I'd always wanted to be. Which became both what I enjoyed most about the Philippines and missed about life in India. I missed the attention of my parents, which seemed to have irrevocably shifted. I missed the family I had left behind – uncles and aunts and cousins and grandparents, but most of all, my beloved great-grandfather, who in his eighties had remained sprightly and fun, but also wise. It was *that* ageing grace – of old houses in Kolkata, their heavy furniture and dusty books, but even more, of lined faces and time-softened hands that fed and held and guided – that was absent.

In the Philippines, this was replaced by the gleam of the new and exciting. And an American buoyancy, because in the eighties you could be forgiven for thinking Manila was an American city. The Philippines had been virtually run by the Americans since World War II. Before that the Spanish had colonized them with centuries of deep religiosity. And cruelty. As a result, however, Christmas was flamboyant and loads of fun, and architecture too, had a gracious Mediterranean feel in the older towns and neighbourhoods. On one of our rambles through an old town, I remember happening upon a colonial home with a palm-choked marble bathroom. As big as a hall, it had at its centre not one lacquered commode but two, with a jade and jet chess set between them.

The Latin influence was to be found in their music too, which they loved, breaking into peppy performances at the drop of a castanet. In the eighties, this love for music meant that American pop songs were ubiquitous, and the soundtrack to my growing years consisted of Michael Jackson, Prince, Madonna, Billy Joel, and Bruce Springsteen. Then there was this ridiculous range of mouth-watering ice cream flavours unlike any we'd tasted before. So dazzled was my mother by the delights on offer at the very first ice cream parlour we tried, she ordered too much, and we embarrassingly ended up taking it home in tubs.

On the weekends, we visited the golden beaches, with their long stretches of sea and sand and sky, the anticipation of which kept me going through the week. At school, I flourished academically but was plagued by bullies who targeted me for my quiet (aka 'weird') ways and colour of skin. In one incident etched on my mind – and the reason I fiercely fight bullying now, as a mother, citizen, and artist – I was chased around the schoolyard by a boy with a knife. He was a 'Mestizo', mixed-race, and not entirely accepted by either side, a hurt sometimes offloaded on other children. And small, dark ones were always fair game. This boy called Mike had a Filipino mom, and an American dad he didn't know, so he turned his ire on me. 'What is the colour of Indian blood?' he cried, as he waved his weapon in my face.

The school had a long field bordered with trees I would hide in to dream in the breaks between classes. Until Mike found me. It was also the only school I have ever attended that had its own movie theatre (and its own fairground, with Disney-style rides in the summer). I have always loved stories, and every Friday we were transported in the cool of a proper cinema hall to another world. The movie I can recall most vividly was the spooky *The Watcher in the Woods*, with a dreamy but uneasy feel to it that captured my Manila sojourn most perfectly.

By the end of that first season of movies, I knew I wanted to be a film director. But, in the short term, I could content myself with being a bottle collector, which was a job on offer after each showing. I collected and handed the bottles in for a few pesos that summer quite happily because it allowed me to spend more time in and around the movie hall, dreaming of something better awaiting me. That something was not at the small Southern American café called Tom Sawyer just outside our neighbourhood that I was drawn to, but since my pocket money didn't stretch that far and our cook did a good fried chicken at home, I never went farther than this strange Louisiana diner's swinging front door.

Everything was strange and new, and not only to me. We had only the vaguest idea about Halloween. For our first one there, not long after settling into our new house, Ma was seen planning a party for the local kids who, she'd been told, were coming round for treats. 'What a splendid opportunity for you to make friends!' my mother trilled, filling the house with themed balloons, fragrant brownies, and giant pots of spaghetti that could have fed the entire locality. Even worse, she made us dress in costumes, the scariest parts of which were our natural scowls. We waited and waited for the children that afternoon, as the food and decor wilted, and my mother hid a tear or two.

Then late in the evening the bell rang, to reveal a sea of frightening faces at our door. The Trick or Treaters had left our house for last, as they'd heard of the goodies on offer, working their way to us at the end of the night. Seeing them on the doorstep with their palms out, my mother realized it wouldn't be the party she'd planned, but it could still be the ice-breaker she desired. So, with a smile, she set about doling out spaghetti in paper cups, with wedges of gooey brownie balanced atop. As word got round, wave upon wave of spectres beat a path to our door, petering out finally in the witching hour. The misunderstanding had morphed into a triumph.

On school holidays, we would troop into our blue Ford Escort with our super-excited mutt Popsi, who sensed an adventure in the offing. Heading out early, through quiet avenues to the sea, we'd find the golden sand undisturbed and the warm water shimmering sleepily. We might have a dip and a splash around, with most of the waves generated by Popsi. Or occasionally we'd spot a glass-bottomed boat awaiting passengers and jump on to see the glorious fish. Swimming freely in the sea as we sat constrained by the vessel would be yellow, orange and purple fish, fish with frilly gills, or spotted backs and stripey crests. There were big fish and small fish, fat fish, and thin eel-like ones. There were fish that looked like they should be in *Nemo*, and those better suited to *Jaws*.

Sometimes, we set off for overnight stays farther away. At places like Ilocos Sur, Ilocos Norte or Pagsanjan, we would rent balmy beach cottages made of seasalt and bamboo. In the evenings, we could walk along the shore and find ourselves at a barbecue, to which we'd be warmly welcomed. After generous helpings of chicken adobo, minced pork lumpias, and occasionally lechon (roast suckling pig), there would be bonfires and Pinoy music. Listening from a distance till our heads began to nod, we would meander back to our holiday hut.

Then my beloved great-grandfather died, and the light seemed to go out of our Manila sojourn, and indeed, my life, for a while. He may not have been with me during those painful growing years, but the thought of his loving presence had kept me going through many calamities. We had kept up a steady stream of missives, though there was neither text nor email back then. But we had letters, and books we both loved, that we read together in different parts of the world. And we had wonderful memories of walks around lakes, eclipses spent together, stories and chocolates shared. Pictures I drew for him, and poems he wrote for me.

On our last visit to Kolkata, he was already ailing and not his sprightly self any more; yet, despite the agony of his terminal cancer, he talked to me with all the enthusiasm he had always mustered. When he passed away, a few months after we'd returned to Manila, I couldn't believe he had gone, and for a long while pretended he hadn't. It was not that different from our many years of separation across the oceans. I could talk to him like I always had, in my head and heart, far from the real world and prying ears. Even now he walks with me when I'm alone. Around lakes, and down uneven streets, on which I hear his cane tapping. But especially on beaches. Even now, the swish of a calm sea comes to me in his poet's voice. In fact, if you visit a beach outside Manila now, you might just see a little chocolate-coloured girl with her rather dapper great-granddad walking along the sand.

Is it any wonder the sea means so much to me?

Pause for Thought: The Best Exotic Literary Tour Company

'When both you and I retire, we should start a literary tour company and go tootling across the world in a little white van, or narrowboat, or anything at all that will get us from A to B zestfully!'

It was not the first time I'd made this pronouncement to my husband, but it was never said very seriously. Retirement seemed far away, and anyway, writers die in the saddle. But as they can also write in the saddle, or on any ride at all, it should be perfectly possible to both run a literary tour company and continue writing. The problem with the idea was really that we weren't business-minded at all, and would probably just go off on literary rambles by ourselves, without too much organization, as and when the mood grabbed us. We had, for example, long been planning to traipse to Tuscany on which so many books were based – from *A Room with a View* to *My Italian Bulldozer*. Closer to home, I had every intention of getting my family on a narrowboat to navigate Britain's storied canals together, much in the manner of *Three Men in a Boat*. That was just the start of a very long list of literary locations to tour, one which we'd perhaps never complete but have a blast trying.

Because, just like travel needs to be about relaxation, and sometimes about the forging, deepening or rejuvenation of relationships, once in a while it ought to be about adventure. Adventure comes in many shapes and sizes, and is never one-size-fits-all. If you enjoy mountains and waterfalls but don't want to climb up or jump down them, choose a cabin in the hills from where you can sit and watch them, and have your fill of both. Our own adventures, the ones by design and not stumbled into accidentally, have often been literary. These seemingly staid outings have led us off the beaten track, opening us up to new experiences, including the occasional spot of peril. Because when you go in search of the places that have inspired authors to write stories of suspense, mystery, and drama, well, you get what you ask for.

'We know how to have a rollicking literary adventure, we might even know how to tempt other people on them, but would we know how to keep 'em out of trouble, landing in it as often as we do?' asked the husband with a rueful grin. In response to which I sighed, but with a distinct lack of disappointment. Neither of us would have any regrets if we never acquired a little white van like Mma Ramotswe's with its name emblazoned on its side – the Number 1 Literary Tour Agency. Or The Best Exotic Literary Tour Company. Further suggestions are welcome too, even if we never start that firm. Or get that van! But literary adventures we've had by the vanload and mean to carry on having. It is in the balance between the chilled, impassioned, and totally accidental that we find that perfect trip. And indeed, life.

13

England and Wales
The Game Is Afoot

The door swung open slowly to reveal a tall, bony man standing in the hallway. Long, stringy hair and steel-rimmed glasses framed a cadaverous face. The gloom outside, dark as night on a sodden afternoon in Wales, reflected our own anxiety and the grim expression on the face of the man scrutinizing us. We huddled closer together. Did he think we were intruders?

His housekeeper, rather forbidding herself, had ushered us into this parlour when we knocked on the imposing front door, after a rain-lashed drive through the bottle-green lanes of the Welsh countryside. In the distance, we could hear the plaintive howl of a very large dog.

The man's stony look softened into bewilderment. 'This is Baskerville Hall, my home,' he grated. 'Were you looking for me?' As I stuttered about how we were admirers of Arthur Conan Doyle on a Sherlockian quest, his face suddenly brightened. 'Care for some tea?' he smiled.

My husband and I have often dined out on this story. In our decade of companionable travel, we have amassed a wealth of such tales – funny, scary, moving, and those to do with Sherlock Holmes. At the heart of our shared love of whodunits is an enduring affection for Arthur Conan Doyle's master sleuth. Over the years, we have visited many places connected to Sherlock's adventures, but rarely by design. Like Arthur Conan Doyle who travelled extensively, setting his stories against the many glorious backdrops this small island has to offer, we enjoy exploring Britain. Ever so often, as a result, we have found ourselves traversing Britain in search of Sherlock.

In Ross-on-Wye, a historic English market town on the border with Wales, for a relaxed week in a thatch-roofed cottage and not a Holmesian thought in our heads, we planned to explore the wilderness around us, with its thickets of tall trees, herds of deer and wild boar, and hilltop views. Wandering around the town, we picked up a French loaf, thick slices of ham, and a large bag of freshly picked cherries from the medieval market hall in the centre, for a picnic on a bench under a flowering tree from which we could watch waterfowl and rowing boats on the River Wye, as well as the action on the cricket pitch. As clouds wafted past the church steeple, we mapped out the next few days. We were just an hour's drive from quaint Hay-on-Wye, famous for its teeming bookstores and even busier literature festival. Hurtling through impossibly narrow country lanes to catch

Sting's memoir launch the next day, we spent hours exploring book-choked streets and, afterwards, sampling game pies at creaking country inns.

There was more excitement in store for us at Ross. We had chosen this quiet corner of England for its sylvan beauty, but soon stumbled upon not one, but two, rarely seen Sherlock sites. Conan Doyle, we discovered, had set *The Boscombe Valley Mystery* in the Forest of Dean, the lush woodland around Ross. This short mystery, published in 1891, is a moody tale of murder, revenge, and the redemptive power of love. We set out one sunny morning to find Boscombe Pool, where John Turner had murdered his old Antipodean confederate, Charles McCarthy. We knew there weren't any natural pools in this area, but there were wide bends in the River Wye running through the forest, which resembled pools in their depth and mottled hue. Arriving at the one most often thought to be 'Boscombe Pool', we sat down on its deserted bank to catch our breath. Suddenly, the perfect silence was broken by a flock of birds disturbed from their lair, and behind them, a happy rambler, whistling the opening credits to Jeremy Brett's *Sherlock Holmes*. He stopped when he saw us. 'Did you know that Baskerville Hall is just across the border, only a few miles away?' he asked, uncannily sure of our interest. After his departure, I asked my husband how a stranger could have sized us up so quickly. Elementary, teased Mr Handley. A deerstalker cap will give you away every time.

That afternoon, we found ourselves driving up a windswept rise, to the dark mass of the mansion atop it, crouched against the lashing wind like a large dog. Conan Doyle is believed to

have been a frequent guest of the Baskervilles of Baskerville
Hall, built in 1839. On his visits, he learnt of the local legend
of the hound of the Baskervilles, and scribbling in his journal
on nearby Hergest Ridge, he made it his own. But at the
request of his friends, he set the story in the faraway southern
county of Devon 'to ward off tourists'. On the day we visited,
though the sign swinging in the wind said it was a hotel, it
had all the atmosphere of Conan Doyle's Baskerville Hall –
shuttered, silent, and more than a little sinister. Our encounter
with its owner started on an equally ominous note. So baleful
was the man's scrutiny, we worried that we were about to
become his dog's (a large one by the sounds of it) dinner.
Instead, much to our surprise, we were invited to dinner. And
all because I had uttered the magic word: 'Sherlock'.

Not surprisingly, the next year found us in the bleak Devon
moors where Conan Doyle had transplanted the Baskerville
tale. Keen to experience Holmes and Watson's chase across
dark and dangerous Dartmoor, we set out in the gloaming in
search of the path they'd taken for that climactic scene. To our
delight, at twilight, modern-day Dartmoor looked no different
from its whodunit avatar. Our delight didn't last as the terrain
got tougher to negotiate. As the darkening sky fused with the
black granite of the moors, it wasn't hard to imagine a large,
black dog lying in wait for us in the gloom.

We staggered over rocky ridges known as 'tors', more
interested in returning to our warm inn and perfect coastal
dinner of smoked haddock with sautéed potatoes, than finding
that mythical path. We certainly did not want to stumble
upon Great Grimpen Mire where Stapleton met his end.

Luckily for us, it hadn't rained in a few days, and bogs only form when torrents of rain mix with spongy Dartmoor peat. The next morning, after a hearty English breakfast, we resumed our search for Fox Tor Mire on which Conan Doyle based his beastly bog. Driving as close to it as we could, we got a tor-top view of that famous marsh into which you could disappear forever and never look upon another Sherlock setting again.

From Devon we travelled to its sister county of Cornwall. Daphne du Maurier had found its dramatic rocky beaches with secret coves and low-wheeling seabirds the perfect locale for her passionate novel, *Jamaica Inn*. The ferocity of the crashing waves would have reminded her of the lives lost on these stony Cornish shores when ships ran aground, and become the backdrop to her story. But Conan Doyle's tale of a murdered family, *The Adventure of the Devil's Foot*, was set inland in a little Cornish village he called Tredannick Wollas. At the real Predannack Wollas, a stunning coastal walk with little hamlets dotted around it, we found the scenery he had in mind when he wrote that eerie account of an unusual poisoning. It was charming in the sunshine but chilling when dusk descended and the mists rolled in, when all you could hear were the moaning waves and the drip of rainfall.

Of course, no Sherlockian tour is complete without a trip to London, Holmes's hometown and scene of many of his deductive triumphs. Sherlock, as everyone knows, lived at 221B Baker Street. Benedict Cumberbatch made it his home in the recent BBC series, *Sherlock*. But before that, there was the equally accomplished Jeremy Brett, and a whole host of other, lesser Sherlocks. And if you are a fan of Holmes and Watson, where else would you go? Taking a detour through Soho – where Conan Doyle based a seamy scene or two, and Cumberbatch in *The Blind Banker* discovered a deadly oriental crime syndicate – we walked through the ornate Chinese gate, past a long row of tempting Chinese restaurants, scanning their upper storeys for unlikely signs of opium dens and hideouts for the Black Lotus Gang. We soon settled for the pleasures of an aromatic Asian meal over an afternoon spent pretend-sleuthing. Then it was time to visit that Georgian house on Baker Street.

With the exception of a sign outside, there is nothing to suggest that this is a treasured British establishment and huge tourist draw. It is discreet, as the residence of a private eye should be. Its place, next to the most restful park in the city, gives it a certain serenity. There's always more of a throng around Holmes's statue at the Baker Street tube station just down the road. Inside, the house is usually abuzz with tourists on a busy day, but on that unseasonably arctic weekday afternoon, there was a hush, a chance to browse quietly. Surrounded by the minutiae of Sherlock's life we'd been familiar with since childhood, we felt immediately at home.

But looking through keepsakes from his cases, a particular exhibit intrigued us – a pipe we could have sworn Sherlock never smoked. We scanned the room for a guide who might cast some light on this mystery. Unable to spot a single official soul, our eyes alighted on the little old lady hovering near Sherlock's desk, almost as if she were contemplating a spot of dusting. We've often found that fellow enthusiasts know as much as guides, so we asked her about the perplexing pipe. Smiling kindly, she agreed that it was a most mysterious pipe, belonging to anyone from Mycroft to Moriarty, but by virtue of its enigmatic origins, it merited a place at 221B Baker Street. Her tale was peppered with details that only an intimate of Sherlock's could know.

'Thank you,' I said, as I turned to leave, 'Ms...?'

'Mrs Hudson, of course,' she threw over her shoulder as she disappeared into the gloom of a corridor leading into the house.

Out on the street, we dissolved into delighted laughter. It had to be her. Who else would know Holmes so well? And with the happy thought that we'd been given a rare insight into our favourite sleuth by his devoted housekeeper, we took ourselves off to the Sherlock Holmes Pub, a tube ride away at Charing Cross, for a special Sherlockian 'one for the road' before our night train to Nottingham.

14

Dorset

Four Go Off in a Caravan

As a five-year-old in Kolkata, I scrutinized one picture every day. Tucked away in a motley but magical collection of Enid Blyton stories, it showed a couple of running children, their rosy faces alight with excitement. Their dog scampers alongside them, scuffing up the pristine sand as it goes. A picnic hamper lies open and depleted, every last crumb of buttered scone and drop of ginger beer gone. A radiant sun watches over them.

I spent as many hours reading about splendid seaside trips, enchanted wishing chairs, and the exciting adventures of a gypsy caravan stowaway, as I did poring over the pictures in those books. Together, the words and images stoked my already-crackling imagination. I conjured up a world where the sun always shone (never scorched), picnics happened every day, wishes came true, and everyone had a bosom buddy. I liked this world. I wanted more of it.

One tale particularly caught my fancy, a mystery surrounding a crumbling hilltop castle – Kirrin – silhouetted against a bright new moon as four children and a dog scramble towards it. I carried this image with me into adulthood just as surely as I retained a small stash of much-loved books, saving them from the wilting heat, termite hordes, and monsoon floods of my Kolkata years for my children of tomorrow.

When my son turned five (and my wise-beyond-her-years daughter, three), it was time to hand over my hoard of magical getaways to the new dreamers. As the days grew warmer in the spring, we sat in our foxglove-smothered garden in Nottingham, lost in these wondrous other worlds till tea time.

Imagine our delight when one day, we discovered that Kirrin Castle not only existed, it was just four hours away. A soaring eleventh-century ruin in the coastal village of Corfe in Dorset, in southern England, was the basis for Blyton's castle. Dorset beaches, we also learnt, had the silvery sands of the treasured sketches of my first book. As if storybook beaches and a ruined castle weren't enough, a tiny shop of Enid Blyton curios in Corfe boasted of the last of the politically incorrect golliwogs, banished from the rest of England.

There was another compelling reason to visit Dorset. Thomas Hardy, a favourite author from my university years, had written his searing tales of love and loss in this corner of England. Our minds were made up. Alongside our Enid Blyton adventure, we would go hunting for Hardy's world of never-ending fields under big sky and mellow sun, of thatched cottages, and the primeval men and women he immortalized in prose and poetry.

But the most exciting aspect of our trip was kept a secret from the children.

Our drive down to Dorset on a sunny Saturday was the usual mix of goofy games, unplanned stops for chocolate cravings, and my-head-feels-wobbly moments. At journey's end was a patch of green in which stood, to the amazement of our young 'uns, a gleaming motor home, a modern take on the brightly painted gypsy caravans they so adored.

With whoops of joy, they ran in to explore. In the space of nine metres, there was everything you could want on holiday: kitchenette, bathroom, four beds that were sofas by day, and even a dining table. The rainproof awning would allow us alfresco meals, whatever the weather.

That was a week ago. Tonight, we are celebrating the conclusion of our gloriously literary holiday with one more storybook standard: a campfire dinner. While Daddy heats the chilli-spiked baked beans, I skewer the sausages for the kids to cook over the fire. There are buttered French loaves and cuts of ham. The pièce de résistance is a tub of gooey-sweet marshmallows for toasting under the stars, with a swap-a-story session to wrap up the holiday.

Our little boy pipes up, 'I'm glad we went to Corfe Castle first, Mommy. Holidays can start slow but ours began with the best!'

Syon loves castles of all sorts, but crumbling remains are 'tops' because they can be mentally refashioned to his satisfaction, with dreadful dragons in deep wells and battle-ready longbow men bristling on the ramparts.

My castle-combing children had got busy the minute we had arrived. They marvelled at the dizzyingly high towers and turrets. They weaved in and out of the rubble, and ran up steep stone steps (to my consternation). Corfe, the signs told us, was built by the mighty Norman William the Conqueror. When razed in the English Civil War, a forgotten Saxon stronghold was discovered underneath. When we visited, the castle was celebrating its antiquity with a Saxon fair that appeared to have emerged from the mists of time. Packs of people in period-costumes thronged pottery and trinket stalls. At a dressing-up booth for children, Syon snapped up the chance to be a knight, but his fastidious sister turned her nose up at the finery on offer. The high point of the day for our little boy was the mock battle on the castle green, with its stirring swordplay and martial stunts.

At the campfire, Ayana rolls her eyes at her brother's tale of derring-do. 'Castles are fine for boys but there's nothing quite like the smell of the sea,' she enunciates precisely.

Our next stop had been the seaside. The sun was blazing, the sea the brightest blue, and the sand shimmered with sea-tossed treasure: crabs, clams, clusters of seaweed, and seashells of every shade. The beach teemed with sun-worshippers, sand-sculpting children, and their shaggy dogs. Sandcastle-building is a competitive sport for English kids, so mine got to work straightaway. Our little girl's dainty fairy palace was bested on this occasion by her brother's sprawling effort with bulwarks, buttresses, and a striking resemblance to Corfe, but the day had just begun.

With a break for blueberry ice cream, and a dip in the mirror-clear sea, the beach games continued. The kids waded gingerly in rock pools amongst the fish, shellfish, and marine plants. At their father's behest, they threw back the shuffling little crabs they had netted. This challenge was about to end in a draw when Ayana spotted a most unusual creature nestling at the bottom of a pool. 'I've found a teeny-weeny shoe, Daddy,' she declared. 'Syon has only found a crab. I bag this round.'

Back at the campfire, both children want to recount our tour of bloodthirsty Henry VIII's formidable harbour fort, Portland Castle, when Daddy settles the matter amicably by making it his story.

The sea was a brilliant blue once again. The deep-walled Tudor fortress was a dream come true for a battle-hungry boy (and his rowdy-at-times sister). They spent a happy afternoon scrambling up cannons, examining yellowed maps, and trying on a battery of bellicose naval helmets. Driving to the highest bluff for a picnic afterwards, we were met with an unforgettable view of Dorset's white sand coast, pretty fishing villages, and bustling harbours.

It is my turn to tell a tale. As the campfire dances, I retrace the steps of my hunt for Hardy.

We took the green-gold steam train from Corfe to Dorchester, chugging through Thomas Hardy country, to discover how much of his world survives in modern-day Dorset.

Dorchester was a disappointment. But for one stately home purportedly belonging to the Mayor of Casterbridge, the town had none of the atmosphere I sought. Instead, we found the best little bakery in Dorset in a serpentine alley. Filling our hamper with chilli-cheese scones and apple-cinnamon cake, we made our way to gracious Max Gate, Hardy's last home. It is the delight Dorchester wasn't. We were immediately adopted as honorary Hardies and lavished with tea, cakes, and attention, followed by Maypole dancing with the local women, and our Dorchester-bought lunch under Hardy's favourite tree.

The train then took us to a sleepy station at the entrance to the woods that inspired Hardy's *Under the Greenwood Tree*. Following the winding path to his birthplace, our eyes alighted on the prettiest thatched cottage we had seen in a decade of thatched-cottage-sighting. Set in an overgrown garden of apple trees and bluebells, the cottage is redolent with the life of those times. For the briefest of moments, as I sat at his writing desk and looked out on his view, I felt an urge to write poetry. It passed. But I came away convinced that Hardy's world of brooding passion lived on in Dorset, in its ancient forests, and fathomless blue sea.

There is still the story of the shoe to be told and the children clamour for it. But it's getting late, and as their father puts out the fire, I herd them in. In the comfort of the caravan kitchen, we sit down with milk and cookies to discuss this last day of our holiday and that mysterious miniature shoe.

Clutching the shoe, Ayana takes us back to Corfe, in the shadow of the castle. We were looking for the Enid Blyton curio shop. We had been told it had a wishing chair, and the kids were convinced that a wish to find the owner of the shoe would lead us to them. The village itself was straight out of my picture books. From the quaint clusters of cottages to the huddle of shops (a sweet shop, a cake shop, and a dressing-up shop), we could easily have stepped into a Famous Five or Malory Towers adventure.

Outside the tiny shop, the enchanted chair sat in the fading afternoon sun. Squeaking with excitement, the children jumped in, and squeezing their eyes tightly shut, made their wish. Immediately, a head poked out of the shop, asking them in. We gazed in wonder at the shelves stacked high with rarities: mint-condition copies of vintage Blyton, handcrafted toys, and in the corner, with ear-to-ear grins on their flat, dark faces, a whole row of dangerously subversive golliwogs. Having only ever read about them, the children approached them with a healthy dose of caution. Till Ayana gasped, 'One's missing a shoe!' Sure enough, one golly in a blue and red tux had only one shoe. Almost reverently, Syon slipped on the lost shoe. It fitted.

Hard-hearted though we felt, we explained to our children that Golly and his reunited shoe could not come home with us. There in that quaint corner of Dorset, surrounded by his kin, was where he had to stay. Turning to look at the shop of wonders one last time as I led the children out, I saw Missing Shoe Golly raise his arm in farewell to us.

'I saw it too, Mommy,' my little boy whispers in my ear, as I tuck him into his caravan bed the last time on this trip. Half an hour later, they are both asleep, with smiles on their lips.

15

Haworth
Wuthering Heights

The North Yorkshire moors are as much of a living, breathing entity now, as they were when the passionate and brooding Brontës lived amidst them. The moors, like the Brontës themselves, are primeval in the force and fluidity of their moods. When the sun shines, and a gentle breeze blows through the heather, gorse and long grass, rippling green, gold and purple in the light, it's all liquid air and luminous colours, as if the cares of the world can't touch their ancient sweep. But these are rare interludes, and the moors at night or in inclement weather are forbidding.

Darkly opaque and oppressive, the moors can turn into a slavering beast, especially when a constant rain transforms large tracts into treacherous swamps. And in strong wind and storm, they become the embodiment of elemental passion and its inevitable destruction, which defined the lives and works of the Brontës.

Emily was channelling the power of the landscape that gave them breath and inspiration, when she professed in *Wuthering Heights*, 'My love for Linton is like the foliage in the woods: time will change it, I'm well aware, as winter changes the trees. My love for Heathcliff resembles the eternal rocks beneath: a source of little visible delight, but necessary.' And so was Charlotte when she declared in *Jane Eyre*, 'I am not an angel … and I will not be one till I die: I will be myself. Mr Rochester, you must neither expect nor exact anything celestial of me – for you will not get it.'

Trekking through these stunning vistas on a clear autumn day, we see none of the danger and darkness, just technicolour scrub and bright blue skies. Our long, bracing walk, with many diversions along the way – from the replica Brontë parsonage set up for the BBC film *To Walk Invisible*, to encounters with fat, happy sheep, to moments of unabashed amazement at the beauty around us – brings us to the pretty village of Haworth where the Brontës spent much of their lives. We know it to be pretty because we've been here before, but approaching it from the back, we find ourselves at their austere parsonage first – the shuttered school beside it and the spectacularly spooky cemetery in front. Haworth, from where we stand, is more bleak than beautiful.

Stepping into the house, now a museum dedicated to the lives and works of the Brontës, we feel a mix of awe and pity. Fabulous women of prodigious talents lived here, to which every room and exhibit bear testimony. Be it the clean lines of their spartan furniture, the reams of fantastic writing they produced as children, or their letters to each other, revealing their innermost thoughts. This last saddens as much as it impresses, just like the chair where young Emily spent her last writing days, and Branwell's portentous painting in which he is blotted out.

But beyond the memento mori of remarkable lives snuffed out too soon, there is a profound silence. 'Silence is of different kinds, and breathes different meanings,' Charlotte mused in *Villette*.

And it's true; the almost elevating hush of the house is different from the meaner silence of the neighbouring Sunday school with its cold, comfortless classrooms, where Charlotte taught briefly till writing success allowed her to escape teaching altogether. 'I scarcely knew what school was; Bessie sometimes spoke of it as a place where young ladies sat in the stocks, wore backboards, and were expected to be exceedingly genteel and precise.' This muteness too is distinct from the unnerving, lull-before-the-storm stillness of the Gothic cemetery at the foot of the parsonage, where every grave is overlaid with a stone slab, as if in anticipation of the dead rising from their rest.

Once out of the green and pleasant garden, where you can still hear the Brontë children playing in their make-believe worlds of Gondal and Angria, the mood changes quickly. Along the Main Street, Haworth is postcard-pretty with its brightly coloured shop fronts and charming, old-world tea rooms. The elegant antiquarian bookstore in particular grabs our attention. Its window, full of yellowing treasures, draws us in.

As soon as we leave the store, our arms full of literary loot, we are sucked into the seductive sweet shop across the street, which holds as many delights for us as it does for our children. We sidestep the lure of the pub, unlike poor Branwell, of whom Anne may well have been thinking when she wrote, 'I see that a man cannot give himself up to drinking without being miserable one half his days and mad the other,' in *The Tenant of Wildfell Hall*.

Despite the unhappiness, beautiful Haworth, looking now much as it did then, provided what comfort was to be found in the Brontë sisters' lives. They would likely have dropped in to the same upbeat bakery, the same cheerful post office, and the park full of flowers in bloom on their daily rounds. Emily might have stolen away to this very park on a fine day like the one we'd picked to visit, when she wrote, 'Every leaf speaks bliss to me, fluttering from the autumn tree.'

And though the moors gave them far more by way of inspiration, it is here we want to leave these gloriously gifted Brontë women, so passionate, and even compassionate, in the face of tragedy. Here, where there is sunshine and light and merriment – once and for all.

Pause for Thought: Tots Can Trot

What's so different about travelling with children then? Oh, everything! As any parent/grandparent/teacher on a school trip/seriously hands-on uncle or aunt can tell you, travelling with children is a whole different jar of sweets. Our family holidays are hugely enjoyable, though I cannot say they are relaxed. Just chillin' on holiday eludes me at the best of times, but when you have kids along, that's not even an option.

As at home, but even more on holiday where everything is new and exciting or scary, you have to be many things to many people, morphing into new roles every few minutes, with new tasks to execute. You have to be clown and circus ringmaster, chauffeur, cook, and cleaner, guide, nurse, and health and safety officer, teacher, friend, philosopher, and, of course, parent. And that's just the tip of the jobs-list iceberg. Not so different from home after all. But all this in a new setting where you're finding your feet too.

Then there's the generation divide and, in consequence, gulfs in energies and interests. Enough family holidays end with members pulling in different directions to know that that's when you're most likely to spread your waning energies thin. Trying to do everything, or having to settle for only the activities the kids enjoy, or insisting they indulge in yours alone, or when the children are older, splintering into groups and not doing things together as a family at all – these not only cut down on happily engaged family time, the talking at cross purposes (and resultant misunderstandings) multiply too! Trust me, there's NO way you can match your young 'uns for energy, or their ability to mess about, so don't even try…

What we mean when we say...	Young, footloose couple:	Older couple, left to themselves:	Couple with kids:
'Wild'	Painting the town red	Just painting. Or reading. Stationed comfortably at a window by the stormy sea.	'Just because that monkey was swinging from those bars, doesn't mean you have to.'
'Mad'	Looping the loop on a bungee cord	Looping back to holiday haunts you've enjoyed before	Watching *Harry Potter* on a loop on a rainy day in
'Wicked'	What, ahem, happens on holiday stays on holiday…	What happens on holiday, sadly, stays on holiday, e.g., siestas.	'No, you can't take your holiday earthworm collection home.'

What we mean when we say...	Young, footloose couple:	Older couple, left to themselves:	Couple with kids:
'Dirty'	Not illegal but just a bit illicit … clubbing with 'frills'	Not illicit but just a bit ill-advised … clubbing	'Clubbing those Brussels sprouts will not improve their taste (it will, however, make a mess)'.
'Gooey'	Getting creative with food. Finding it in unexpected crevices	Getting creative with food. Finding it on unplanned pit stops	Getting creative with food. Finding it on unplanned pit stops AND unexpected crevices ('Want to see where I put my green peas, Mommy?')
'Sweeet'	Time spent locating that *special* spot	Time spent reminiscing about locating that spot	The relief of locating that runaway tot

So, are calm, happy holidays with children impossible? Far from it. We have them all the time! Less of the calm perhaps and more of the happy, but there are quiet times too, when we come back after a long day's exploring to settle down for the evening with sated kids. And when we are out and about? There's so much to enjoy.

The trick, as any experienced parent will tell you, is to: 1) inculcate a love of the things you adore in your children too. Or if indeed your interests are very different, balance is the key; 2) allocating time for activities that cater to each of you. If it's a theme park you're visiting one day, don't let a few whimpers put you off taking them to art galleries the next, but explain the works of art as you go around, and they'll develop an interest as well.

Of course, time and money are limited, but it is possible to explore new places, enjoy new experiences, and learn new skills, entertaining everyone in the family without it costing the earth. Or indeed, having to travel the earth. Travel to nearby spots of interest or beauty, keep the fancy restaurant for the last night, eat at smaller eateries, or make your own grub from local produce, involving the children in the preparation of these new dishes. It will be messy and chaotic but so much fun, and they'll relish every morsel too. The more you get them involved in activities outside their experience, the fewer tantrums and tears there will be, so lost will they be in wonder. You too will see so much with fresh eyes and immerse yourself in them with added zest. It does require oodles more energy, receptivity, and initiative than we sometimes think we have, but it will all be worth it in the end. There is very little you won't love about holidays with your children, and what you don't love, you'll laugh over afterwards. Promise.

16

Wales

Train to the Top

'Shall we climb Mount Everest, Mommy?' asked our son, after having studied about it in school. He was particularly impressed by the tales of Himalayan hazards and heroism he'd heard, and wanted his own high-octane, high-altitude adventure. Being only nine though, he realized he would need his parents and his equally intrepid seven-year-old sister along, hence the question to me, quite out of the blue, one wintry English morning.

It sounded like a good idea: not the distant Himalayas perhaps for our Blighty-based family, but a British mountain holiday instead of our usual (albeit thoroughly enjoyable) seaside sojourns. So we plumped for a jaunt to Mount Snowdon in the summer, the tallest mountain in Wales and third highest in the UK at 3,560 feet. Besides which, the name itself conjured up such visions of snow-covered summits, majestic slopes, and dizzying passes that the kids couldn't sit still from the excitement of our approaching holiday. *Top Family Trip Tip #1: Natter non-stop about impending adventures, because children enjoy savouring the idea as much as the experience itself!*

But even better was that, dramatic though it sounded, beautiful as it undoubtedly would be, Mount Snowdon was going to be a walk in the park, I figured, compared to a Himalayan climb. And that's just the type of tepid adventure we parents wanted, now that keeping the kiddiewinkles safe at all times was our priority (though going easy on our old bones was tempting too). Therefore, the slopes couldn't be too steep, the weather too inclement, or the fall uncushioned by springy green meadow, if a small tumble were to be taken while winding our placid way up. So, the weather forecast, the gradient of the slopes, and the availability of shelter and washrooms at the top were checked and found satisfactory.

Then the summer was upon us, and with it the need to pack wisely. Children on holiday, as you soon discover, have the boundless appetites of Gremlins at midnight, and have to be fed and watered at regular intervals. And so, our rucksacks, unlike most sensible climbers (those not transporting tots to the top), were stuffed full of biscuits, brie, ginger beer and yes, several copies of Enid Blyton's Famous Five to consult should the going get tough. Who, after all, our daughter asked astutely, would know how to solve the little snarls on a British adventure better than Timmy and George? *Top Tip #2: Consult the kids when you pack your bags; only they know what enchanted and improbable objects they will need on holiday.*

And so we set off, on our idyllic dawdle up the mountains, our prance up picturesque slopes that would put *The Sound of Music*'s Maria's Alpine pirouettes to shame. It would be a cakewalk, not a climb, and certainly no uphill task. Or, that's what I thought. Oh, how wrong I turned out to be (though it did in fact culminate with cake)!

The skittish British weather gods, colluding to turn our holiday on its head, led us far, far off the planned promontory. The Beeb had promised us sunshine, our hiking boots had had little workouts at the Welsh castles – grand Caernarfon and hilltop Harlech – we'd combed on our way, and our binoculars were poised and at the ready for magnificent rises and meadows strewn with lamb. *Top Tip #3: When child is bored or upset, point out bouncing baby animal and all will be well.*

It had been pouring all night however, as it does often in beautifully lush yet undeniably wet Wales. But this round of rainfall had been extraordinarily torrential. In the morning, the clouds hung heavy over flooded ground, promising more rain and forcing us to change from our planned route to the mountains to less-travelled roads. But our aged jalopy, it transpired, was not quite equal to the task, slipping and sliding up slick mountain roads before we decided to abandon it altogether. That proved to be providential, as unexpected turns often are on family holidays, because we left it by the most glorious lake, stopping a while to take it in as the sun miraculously peeped out. Before us was a twinkling expanse of turquoise water, with a darker undertow hinting at mysteries beneath, and deep green mountains looming behind.

Lake Cwellyn seemed a scene from a Celtic dream of King Arthur and the Lady of the Lake.

But Snowdon summoned and we dared not tarry. There, however, another obstacle waited. We were informed on arrival that the wind speed had soared to 50 kmph that morning, making an ascent to the summit inadvisable, especially with children in tow. Deeply disappointed, we stood, buffeted by the very winds that would prevent our climb, wondering what to do. Despite our every effort to make it happen, would we have to abandon our long-anticipated mountain adventure after all?

'I hear a chugger, Daddy,' our little girl said just then, pointing to the heritage train station nestling at Snowdon's base. *Top Tip #4: Let your kids' sharper sight and hearing find the silver lining to every washed-out trip; not only will it help you out of a hole, they'll be over-the-moon with it.*

Gathering our rucksacks, children, and hastily bought tickets, we were about to board the historic locomotive when we were stopped yet again. The gale-force gusts assailing the mountains might make it impossible, the conductor warned, for even a sturdy little train like theirs to reach the summit; could we withstand that disappointment? Did we want to take that chance?

We most certainly did! So up we chugged in our ancient yet well-oiled train, with winds whipping around us. Up towards the clouds clustered thickly at the top, where the higher we climbed, the more breathtaking was the view. The mountains morphed from luminous to a sombre, shadowy green. The crags and ridges stood out more proudly. Boulders studded every slope like giants' teeth and the waterfalls roared louder in antipathy. There was even a grey cloud-crowned peak I could have sworn belonged in Mordor. Then, with the wind screaming like a banshee all around us, everything went blank. We had got to the last stage of our ride and were in the clouds.

The train driver clanged his bell and announced that he would have to take a wind reading to see if we could go any farther. An unnatural hush descended on the carriage, even as the weather gods continued bellowing outside. The children's faces fell. Then their heads drooped. And I remembered what we'd brought in our bags – tons and tons of Enid Blyton! So I whipped out *The Magic Faraway Tree* (who knew they'd smuggled that in too) and started reading aloud. They read omnivorously and on their own but this was an emergency. I read about Moonface and Silky, and their adventures in the clouds. I related the delight of the fictional children every time they entered a wonderful new world, while my own listened rapt. *Top Tip #5: Ain't a child who doesn't love a story, so keep 'em handy.*

The train driver, in the meantime, had finished his wind check and waved us an all-clear triumphantly. We were on our way to the summit after all! So what if we were so lost in billows of white we could barely see? We were chugging up that last incline and totally chuffed.

True to form on that trip, we could see nothing at the top either. Our dream of viewing wondrous, verdant Wales in all its glory from Snowdon's summit was dashed, as we'd suspected it would be. Dark, wet, and gusty at its crest, we had no choice but to board our train again and head down to the dramatically forked Rhyd-Ddu Path near which we'd left our car.

In the end though, it was neither an anti-climax nor a disappointment. We did get to the top. And what a glorious ride it was, with magnificent vistas to be spied on either side as the train trundled on. But like every family film and fairy tale, the best had been saved for last. At journey's end in teeny, tiny Rhyd-Ddu, we stopped for a snack in the only shop in town, Ty Mawr. And in that charmingly homely, higgledy-piggledy café, we found the kind of adventure we'd been looking for all day. With no peaks and no troughs, and not a smidgeon of scary, it came chocolate-laden, apple-topped, or oozing honey. Large, flat, round, and hot, they were just what we needed after our nippy exploits at the top. Here were crêpes to equal Daddy's Shrove Tuesday pancakes, and we talked about them long after our summit attempt had been forgotten. *Top Tip #6: A tummy full of good food, we've found, is all the adventure kids need sometimes.*

That is, till we got back home and my son piped up again, 'So, when are we going to the Himalayas, Mommy?'

17

Disneyland, Paris
Never Never Land

Remember the first time you watched a Disney film? You stood in line for your ticket and then for popcorn, with barely contained excitement. Having made it into the hallowed hall, you were led like a traveller across mysterious terrain, by a wondrously sure-footed usher, picking out your seat with a glow-worm torch in that cavernous dark. Remember squirming with anticipation through the seemingly endless pre-film ads? When the main feature finally started, with stirring music and a luminescent castle that filled the vast screen, remember how you wished with all of your earnest five-year-old heart that you could be transported to that magical land?

Dreams do come true. Even the ones you have forgotten. One warm Parisian evening, more than three decades later,

I found myself standing in front of the castle that had haunted my childhood dreams. Sleeping Beauty's castle slumbered, its delicately pointed spires wrapped in the midnight-blue velvet of the night, as we positioned ourselves on a grassy knoll to watch the promised magic unfold. It was our last night at Disneyland Paris after a frenetic five days, and we had been assured a fitting finale at the park's centrepiece. As I propped up my four- and six-year-olds so they could see better, my inner child scrambled out too.

With indrawn breath, we watched the most splendid son et lumière; luminous Disney characters fashioned from the interplay of light and occasional jets of water pranced and danced across the castle walls, as familiar songs rang out. The play of coloured lights on the castle kept changing so it looked brooding, then romantic and jolly, as the unfolding story took twists and thrilling turns. Peter Pan lost his rascally shadow, Aladdin took Jasmine on a magic carpet ride, and jovial Jiminy Cricket jigged from turret to turret with a cavalcade of other characters, before giving way to a magnificent fireworks display.

On our slow, contemplative walk back at the end of the show, which was also the end of our holiday, the children asked what I'd liked best. 'Watching you two,' I said quite honestly. Their incandescent happiness had made every spot of bother during the trip worthwhile. In truth, I had worn the same utterly captivated expression on my own face through most of it. For those five days, I had joyously, unapologetically, become five years old again. 'What did you two enjoy most?' I questioned in turn. All of it, they whooped. Every last bit.

And that was what we'd travelled across the Channel for, why we'd spent a tidy sum to vacation in an amusement park (of all places, I'd said to myself in the run-up) instead of a spot of salubrious beauty.

Our Disneyland plan was hatched with another young family at a giant aquarium two years ago. Chickenpox, school admissions, and the detritus of day-to-day life meant it was a while before we found ourselves boarding an early morning train bound for Paris from St Pancras in London. For the children, the adventure began at the Channel crossing, with its thirty-eight-kilometre journey under the sea. Once in Paris, our Indian taxi driver took it upon himself to keep the children entertained with his dashboard-thumping Desi take on classic Disney songs.

As we walked up Main Street, U.S.A. leading to Disneyland Park, we were transported to 1930s' America, a mythical, magical version of it, with seemingly edible candy-coloured houses, and costumed shopkeepers and carriage drivers who beamed at everyone. It was my kind of made-up world, with a real historical basis, and I could have sauntered about all afternoon, scrutinizing vintage signs, peering into shop windows, or watching the world go by from a whitewashed bench. But the children were running on ahead to the largest, most glittering carousel we had ever seen. A soothing, musical merry-go-round ride was followed by a gentle flight through Peter Pan's Never Land with islands, pirates, crocodiles, and J.M. Barrie's famous house in London where it all began. The kids were ready for more audacious experiences, so we hopped on to the Buzz Lightyear Laser Blast, a madcap test of marksmanship in which we aimed to annihilate the baddie Zurg on our tour of the universe. Stepping out we were confronted by the Orbitron, a ride with spaceships that spin you about in the air until you feel just a little bit the worse for wear. The kids, however, loved it.

They could have continued, ride after ride after ride, but the old fogies were beginning to flag. It was also time for the first Disney extravaganza of the trip – the big parade through the heart of the park. 'I hate parades,' sulked six-year-old Syon. 'It'll be full of princesses.' There were princesses aplenty, but also whirling witches, marching toy soldiers, and dancing crockery. Glittering floats full of beloved Disney heroes, featuring scenes from the movies sailed past us. Long lines of colourful, energetic characters followed in their wake. Ayana, our four-year-old, let off peals of delighted laughter as Belle took time out from waltzing with the Beast to give our little girl a squeeze.

The floats kept coming. Venerable, pointy-hatted Merlin on his spangled platform was followed by a golden pumpkin with Cinderella and Prince Charming aboard. Tree houses, twee cottages, and Indian jungles later, the eagerly awaited final float coasted past with Donald, Goofy, Pluto, Minnie, and Mickey atop. The last, in his wizarding robes from *The Sorcerer's Apprentice*, stirred up a storm in his cauldron, with a sprinkling of magic and a dash of mayhem for good measure. As he swept past, flames shot out from the big brass crock, surprising us all.

Like the heady mix in Mickey's cauldron, Disneyland turned out to be a fine blend of magic and mayhem. The latter took hold the day we visited the neighbouring Walt Disney Studios. We found the magic curiously missing. It lacked the affable charm of its sister park: the lines were longer, making the children chafe, and the attendants ruder, curtly answering questions about the many closed attractions. A number of times we struggled to the end of an hour-long line only to be told the ride had broken down. We even found ourselves stranded high in the sky when the *Toy Story* parachute-ride malfunctioned in mid-air. Fortunately for us, our kids view nearly everything as an adventure and so were neither scared nor bored. They kept us all entertained with cheery speculation about the size of the splat we would make, if we slipped from our harnesses and fell to the ground. Happily, this remained conjecture. Other disappointments awaited us though, the biggest being the tram tour of the studio. Meant to be an awe-inspiring guide to the mechanics of moviemaking, it induced less awe and more shock as incredibly little happened.

But the day was about to get better. A car stunt show involving dazzling daredevilry in a giant arena entranced the children. The set, done up to resemble a sleepy street in Italy, intrigued me. And the best bit had been saved for last. We went to visit (hold your breath because our gaggle of kids certainly did) Spiderman! Our son had dressed the part, adding to the confusion of the younger children there. 'So, if Spiderman's in there,' whispered one little boy to his mother, pointing to the closed studio doors, 'who is this?' After a two-hour wait in the sun, we were admitted into the presence of the great man. No sooner had we entered, were we swept into the long, all-encompassing arms of a man who chattered non-stop about saving New York and letting my identically dressed son take over in a few short years. After some web-spinning training and photographs, we went home happy with what we'd seen. And that included the amazing abs (and more) of which the ladies in our line had tipped me off.

Not everything went swimmingly in Disneyland Park either. The *Pirates of the Caribbean* ride had loads of atmosphere with its dimly lit labyrinth of subterranean tunnels leading to a wild boat ride over rapids, round buccaneering islands and caves full of treasure, but the children hated it. Our friends' son dissolved into tears after the umpteenth drenching. Thunder Mountain, a Wild West themed super-speedy rollercoaster ride led to another bout of tears, not from Syon who revelled in every screeching, careening moment of it, but his younger sister who was too young to be allowed on. As consolation, I took her on an Adventure Land mini cruise instead, on a big paddle steamer with views of frontier homesteads, gunslingers, and wild moose, plying her with sweets as we went. But it was all in vain as she wept through the journey.

The worst happened, however, when we lost her for a heart-stopping few minutes in Alice's Curious Labyrinth. Every parent knows what this feels like. When you realize that that little hand is no longer safely slipped into yours, the mind races even as the heart nearly stops. Your eyes rake the crowds searching for that little red cap, the bright raincoat, the stripey boots you'd slipped them into earlier. We experienced it when a stampeding herd of schoolkids had just passed us, with one of them snagging their bag in the shrubbery. Their teacher, apologizing profusely, had enlisted my husband's help in untangling the bag from the bush. Breathing a sigh of relief when they moved on, we did a head count and came up one short. The sun dipped behind the clouds, and the colourfully surreal maze took on a sinister hue. Telling ourselves that she couldn't have gone far, we struck off in different directions. Gripping her older brother's hand so hard he yelped, I took every twist and turn holding my breath, expecting to come upon my little girl any minute, fearing that I never would. We reached the end of the maze in this panic-stricken state and regrouped. No Ayana.

One of our friends went to inform a park attendant as we scoured the maze again. Suddenly, her brother spied a little gap in the hedge down a path we had already traversed thrice. It could only have been spotted by another child. He tugged at my sleeve wordlessly and slipped in, popping his beaming face out a moment later to whisper, 'She's here.' I squeezed in, being nearly child-sized myself. There, in a little clearing was Ayana in her pretty purple pinafore, the guest of honour at the Mad Hatter's table. She was listening sympathetically to the White Rabbit's plight. She saw us and smiled that smile that melts my heart. This time, especially so. The disused table had been tucked away out of sight of most visitors but Ayana had unearthed it and lost herself in the pleasure of the find.

And so, our penultimate evening ended happily. On our last ride, a slow cruise through a dazzling array of dolls from around the world singing their mechanical hearts out against a vibrant backdrop of famous vistas, we sang along to the rousing strains of 'It's a Small World'. We followed up our full-throated efforts with a celebratory meal at the Rainforest

Café, the kids' restaurant of choice, where we indulged in triple-decker burgers and glorious chocolate concoctions amidst palm trees, fern fronds and gentle cascades, while automated elephants trumpeted, and snakes hissed overhead.

Ayana fixed me with her twinkling eyes and said, 'You know, Mommy, I didn't get to finish my chat with the White Rabbit today, so I was thinking...'

'...that we should return to Disneyland very, very soon,' finished Syon in a green-eyed rush.

Their earnest faces tugged at my heartstrings and I let the five-year-old in me do the talking, one last time that holiday. 'You know what? I loved it too. Come back in a couple of years, shall we?'

Paws for Thought: Our Canine Conundrum

A fter a decade of parenthood, we embarked on a whole new adventure. We couldn't tell you why since we were still reeling from the impact of our children's boundless energies, but we saw a pup on our travels and fell in love with it. We called her Luna, for a host of reasons, but mostly because she displayed all the oddball independence of one of my daughter's favourite fictional characters – the eccentric Luna Lovegood. Our Luna settled down and learnt to love good too. But then came the little matter of reconciling this new love with an old one – travelling.

'How does one go on holiday with a dog?' we asked ourselves.

'Disguise her in a hat and coat maybe?' The daughter smiled.

'We'd have to teach her to stand upright first.' The son laughed back.

'Isn't her booming bark a sure giveaway?' our youngest wondered next.

'No, no, my class teacher sounds exactly like that!' the growing (mischievous-by-the-minute) boy exclaimed.

With that, they both rolled about in a pool of sunlight, on the oak floor of our yellow and blue kitchen, guffawing with their dog. In the glorious sunshine of the summer months in England, we picnic by placid blue lakes and trek through cool green woods on day trips. These we'd already found worked well with the latest member of our clan. But there were others we enjoyed, farther away and for longer whiles, that we didn't know how to pull off with a pup. Having arrived at a no-kennel conclusion, at least while Luna was young and excitable, we didn't know how to keep her close and yet go far. The children chattered on about it, with improbable solutions offered and equally laughingly dismissed. It was the start of spring, and our customary holiday season of springtime and summer were just round the corner.

Our love for sunshine and sun-ripened food had taken us to enchanting France and wondrous Greece in the previous years, before Luna had joined the clan. The memory of those trips made me smile as I flitted between the rooms of our red-brick house, ostensibly busy with my Saturday Tidy: that sweeping away of the children's mess that I threatened all week but only found time to conduct in the weekend when I put away my writing. From the moment our furry bundle of delight arrived, our forest home of over a decade had felt complete. It had always been filled with sunlight and laughter, and the smell of delicious cooking, but now it also smelt of muddy paws and wet ginger biscuits (because, in case you didn't know, that's how a sodden pup smells after a dousing, whether in the bath, or the pond at the bottom of our garden). The first thing we heard with the break of day was the pad of her paws on the floorboards downstairs as she took a round of the house as part of her morning constitutional. Which would then be joined by the children's excited voices, the two together growing in volume till we gave up on sleeping as well.

We had everything we could want right there, and yet, as attached as we were to our haven in the woods, the siren song of other places was heard often, beating a path through the trees to our home. When it rolled up to our door, it was time to set off again. But this time, our itchy feet were beginning to twitch in a world where pets couldn't easily travel.

As I set our house to rights that bright spring morning, picking up and dusting the souvenirs of the very trips on our mind, I couldn't think of a way to do the same with our world. Like the solutions that would not present themselves, a porcelain cow, a miniature of the life-sized fibreglass ones that had dotted Zurich's streets on my visit, nearly gave me the slip, landing safely on the aquamarine rug pooling at my feet. Bending to retrieve it, I heard the pair of wooden penguins we'd acquired at Trouville-sur-Mer hastily totter back to elude my grasp. Our small jade Laughing Buddha appeared to be chuckling at our quandary too. My dusting was clearly not going to make any headway today, I rued, and the little particles dancing in the sun would remain as teasingly out of reach as the answers to our canine conundrum. Where, oh where could we go with our beloved bundle of fluff?

Not anywhere at all in Europe, with its many travel restrictions, and purely for the distance, not back home either. Home was, of course, Sherwood Forest, of jewel-green pines and ruby-red apple orchards. But home was also mishti doi, and Ma-er gaan, on a south Kolkata balcony amidst a jungle of potted palms, elephantine mosquitoes, and the steady tattoo of rain. Strangely taking the path of my own thoughts, I could hear the children chortling about the mischief Luna would get up to if let loose in their Dadu and Didou's Kolkata flat. With great regularity, Luna dug up our garden, tracking mud all over the house, and her greatest joy was bounding into our laps long after she'd outgrown them. Where could we take our madcap, much-loved dog?

From where I stood, I could see not only towering walnut trees and swathes of green grass dipping to meet the ancient wall that marked the end of our property, but also the man with All The Answers. The one who'd never let me down in all our twenty years together. He was smoothing down the springy ribbons of green in the garden with his mower, with the cuddly canine in question loping beside him. As if sensing my warm appraisal, he looked up at just that moment to blow a kiss. This excited the pup however, who jumped on the mower, bringing it to heel. The chatter that had filled the house all morning ground to a halt too as the possibilities dwindled, and the sun outside appeared to dim. A shadow had just crossed its glowing face. It grew and grew till it eclipsed the light in the doorway, our perennially sunny kitchen, even our red-brick home. Then the obscured glass doors swung open, to reveal ... Daddy. And in his arms was a pup more muddy than we'd ever known.

In answer to our stunned questions on Luna's state, Daddy rolled his eyes and pointed to where the moss green forest joined our garden, where the heavy rains of the wet and windy months preceding spring had made a mud-bath out of our shallow pond. There, where Luna dunked herself deliriously when our backs were turned (though never before to such effect), and two magpies and a knot of toads now waited their turn, lay the solution to our holiday puzzle. I turned to my husband with a smile as satisfied as Luna in sludge and proclaimed, 'Muck it is then!'

18

Wye Valley

Puppy Love

Pups love books too. Eating them.

Which is why we had to think twice and then thrice before taking Luna with us on our Wye Valley trip, because a big part of that was going to be the Hay Book Festival that we'd been planning to revisit for all of fourteen years. The River Wye flows through the ancient Forest of Dean, giving life to pretty towns on its banks and watchful castles on hilltops, in this valley shared by England and Wales. Our first holiday as a couple had been spent amongst its historic and bookish delights, but with a wedding and two children and careers that kept us busy, and many other interesting places to holiday in as well, we hadn't had the chance to come back here. But now, with our children growing up as bookish as we were, it was time to return. To picturesque

Ross-on-Wye, bustling Hay, densely green Symond's Yat, and many half-remembered ruins we knew our castle-crazy children (including the curious canine) would love. But the biggest change we would be making on this holiday, for the sake of the children, and even more our dog, was where we would stay. When we'd come to this part of the world on our own, we had rented a romantic barn conversion. A love nest in the eaves of a Tudor homestead, lovingly renovated and smothered in roses. This time, the focus was firmly elsewhere – on all three children having a 'wale' of a time (their favourite joke on the trip!). So we decided to rent a cottage on a farm instead.

The sun was shining on our thatch-roofed cottage for the week when we drove up to it. It was charming in a mired-in-muck kind of way, and its quaint green door, with a friendly bench alongside, to sit and watch the animals or shake the mud off our boots before we stepped in, enhanced the welcome. There were chicken coops up a small swell in front of the cottage. Behind that we could hear a donkey braying, while a sheep dog winked at us from the open barn. 'Ooh, let's go meet them all!' declared our daughter, but was soon distracted by the pitter-patter of tiny cloven feet as a cavalcade of goats rounded the corner to tilt their horned heads, and look at us in surprise. 'If that isn't the goofiest gathering I've ever seen!' exclaimed our son with glee. We all had a thing for goats – for their silly, happy faces, rotund bods, and unexpectedly nimble tread.

All this before we'd even opened the door to our cottage, which we found was really a hobbit hole, with rooms built along a long, dark passage that ran the length of the house.

As the children ran off to bag a bed each, with Luna in the lead, we found our own cosy bedroom, past butter churns, coal scuttles, and mangles that hadn't graced homes since milkmaids became cans. But this was the most singular farm! Even the pictures cluttering the walls were, on examination, quite surreal – most of them clearly done by a painter who loved animals but thought it rude to depict their limbs.

The idea was to have a holiday of two halves. Though every morning started with a scramble up the swell to collect our own eggs from the coops, and a stop at the backdoor of the farmhouse for honey or bacon, as the day wore on it would become a little less homespun, especially if it involved a book festival visit. We knew they didn't allow dogs in, so the plan was that each adult would take their turn at the festival, with a child in tow, to browse, buy, and hear discussions on books, while the other took the second child and the pup into town to explore. But one of us would be getting the better deal, and as I was the first to go to the festival with my daughter, while father and son meandered through the quaint and lovely book village, biding their time, I thought it would be me. We were at the festival that day to see Julia Donaldson's popular children's show, one I'd wanted to watch while both Julia and I had been guest speakers at the Kolkata Literary Meet but couldn't since our sessions had clashed. We had met at the dinner after however, and her husband had very sweetly taken a picture of us drinking.

We arrived to find ourselves at the end of a huge queue waiting to see Julia. The mothers chattered, as the children grazed. Till they were herded away by the same nice man I'd met at the book festival in Kolkata. He was strumming on a guitar and singing funny songs, and soon had all the kids gathered around him, including our little girl, like cuter-than-average rats following the Pied Piper. He led them in song and dance while the mothers had a rest, coming over to say hello afterwards, and that he recognized me. A nice man, I decided, and his wife's show was even nicer, keeping children of all ages enthralled for its entire duration. But the minute we were out, I could see the festival was not the vibrant, free-spirited event it had been when another man had made an impression on me (in an altogether different way).

Fourteen years ago, Sting had been about to enter the big top to talk about his new book *Broken Music*, when he'd stopped a moment to run his eyes over the crowd waiting to hear him. In my early thirties and still alive to such things, I noticed he was taller and handsomer than I'd expected. With the sun falling upon it, his hair seemed spun from gold and without the bald patch that later became so apparent. His broad shoulders looked capable of heroically bearing the world's troubles (or at least several women at a time – his autobiography would suggest he had tried both), and his piercing blue gaze was ... on me! We gazed at each other for what seemed like an eternity, till a guard opened a side gate for him, and the connection snapped. It was then that I realized there was a very large ketchup stain down my front. Had he thought I was dying? Did he not think to try and save me with mouth-to-mouth resuscitation, an unusual staunch though that might seem for blood loss? I was a bit miffed, and with his book turning out to be as beautifully written as it was self-absorbed, I said to myself, 'There, you see, not a thought for anyone other than himself. Not even when they're dying.' And it was a good few months before he was allowed back into my good books again.

With the festival itself proving a soulless disappointment this time, we were happy to head into the quirky, old book town of Hay-on-Wye, where my husband, son, and dog were waiting. And having more fun as it turned out! Here was the kind of book buying we liked to do, with time to canter through cobbled lanes, and spot the best bookshop signs – The Green Ink and The King of Hay, or Outcast and Barna-bee's – and best window displays. At one, I spotted a second-hand (as were most books in Hay) first edition P.G. Wodehouse that I felt compelled to go in and get. That they had the most charming reading nook, with deep armchairs in faded turquoise against a mustard wall plastered with gilt-framed illustrations from much-loved books, helped. As well as a book-lined fireplace that didn't need lighting on that warm summer's day, but looked perfect. Having bought the book and happily skipped out, I was indulgently reminded by my husband that I had bought that very title, *Uncle Fred in the Springtime*, the last time we were there. 'You can never have too many PeeGees!' I laughed, as we moved to another favourite book stop.

Murder and Mayhem, a bijou bookstore dedicated to sleuths, was packed to the rafters with crime fiction books, and a 'crime scene' at the entrance we tiptoed around to avoid disturbing the 'evidence'. On this trip we visited children's bookstores too, including one devoted entirely to comic books, of which our young man had a burgeoning collection. After a long and leisurely browse through every comic in the store, he finally plumped for an early edition of *Superman*. Through it all we kept a firm eye on Luna, allowing her to neither sniff, never mind scoff, the books on show. But in every other way, she fully partook of our holiday – sauntering through the cobbled streets, sitting outside bookstores contentedly, to say hello to the swarms of dogs in town, with whichever one of us was keeping her company.

Between the distinctive bookstores on every street, and thin historic houses, were markets and delis crammed with delights. Although Luna reminded us it was time to eat, with so many festivalgoers scrambling for a spot, it was a while before we settled down to an appetizing North African lunch, and a convivial chat with equally squeezed-for-space strangers. Picking up chicken, cream, and mushrooms at the central market for a stroganoff dinner, we found perches on its sturdy stone walls to watch the sun set on a wonderfully bookish day.

Hay was not the only picturesque town we visited that week. In Ross-on-Wye, with the river wending through it, we sat on a blossoming terrace to watch cricket, with the old castle looming behind us. We drove to Monmouth too, with its historic ruins and riverfront grub, once home to our children's Welsh ancestors, but the *real* fun was waiting for us at the farm.

Just like we'd rubbed shoulders with literary lights at Hay, Luna was keen to roll about *in hay* with the stars of the farm. From the moment we'd arrived, the children had set about making friends with Min-Sing the goat who liked her teatime bickies, Snappy the donkey who expected you to stay a while as he had long, involved tales to tell, and Agatha and Algernon, mother and son sheep, who would harrumph when you swung by, as if your presence was an imposition, yet looked as disconsolate when you made to leave. We agreed what they really needed was a monocle each, but gave them the carrots and celery we fed to all the animals. But the creatures the children adored most were the farm horses: Thorne, Thistle, and Thump. Besides hobnobbing with them, you could also go on guided rides, so the children cantered out on Thistle and Thump halfway through our holiday week, with Luna trotting companionably alongside.

As the children bounced along atop, the conversation between Thump and Luna progressed apace, from pleasantries to histories, such as that time when Luna had found tiny emerald frogs on the patio, and how Thump loved sugar in his lunchtime trough, to deeper, more meaningful stuff they rarely vouchsafed to anyone outside their families. By the time the children's hour-long ride was over, Luna and Thump were BFFs. With Luna throwing herself cheerily back into our activities thereafter – barking happily at Thump when walking past, before settling down with us for delicious dinners, family games and movies, and the animated discussions that led to lights-out every night – we never suspected she was missing her friend.

Then it was time to go. And if we were a wee bit downcast, the weather was worse, drowning the entire valley in its tears that day. Resulting in our last trip to the book festival being washed out in every way, with a dino expert we'd booked to hear not turning up, and a friend we were meant to meet deciding to stay home, despite our long, wet, and windy drive through narrow mountain passes to see them. Poor Luna also had to stay cooped up for most of that day like the chickens outside our cottage. So it was that when we returned – drowned, bedraggled, and battling with our raincoats and wellies to divest ourselves of them as quickly as possible – she took the opportunity to stretch her legs. Racing away with all the swagger of Steve McQueen in *The Great Escape*, Luna disappeared into the rain-obscured horizon, and half-in and half-out of our wet clothing as we were, we followed.

For a good ten minutes, though it felt much longer, we agonized over Luna's safety as we scoured the farm for her. We checked in the barn, the pond, and the long grasses. When Agatha and Algernon gave us sheepish glances, we double-checked to ensure Luna wasn't rolling in their hay. Looking in the pigpen, we were reassured by the pink snouts peeping out, that none of its smelly denizens was our pet. We walked round and round in circles, till it dawned on us that she would have made for the stables. When we got there, wetter than we'd imagined possible, we found a dry, snug Luna curled up with Thump. Both of them munching their way through sugar lumps in the latter's trough. Overcome with relief and love, we could only laugh, though very wet laughs they were too. The next morning found us leaving our hobbit hole, with equally wet noses, stacks of books, jars of farm jam and honey, and wonderful memories of our first holiday with our pup.

19

Whitby

The Wet Dog in the Night-time

On a nippy night in late October, the grand bulk of ancient Whitby Abbey should have been especially beautiful to behold. But it had been hit by an unexpected storm, a surprisingly ferocious one on a night when the most ferocious thing abroad should have been the Dracula actors in their ghoulish gear. It was Halloween, and with Whitby, a small coastal town in North Yorkshire, famous for its stellar role in Bram Stoker's *Dracula*, this was a special night on its calendar. Bram Stoker wrote *Dracula* in 1897, after a visit to Whitby seven years earlier that so impressed him with its eerie atmosphere and chilling stories of shipwrecks, that he set a crucial strand of his Gothic novel in this sea-tossed town. Celebrated on a scale on par with Christmas, every nook and cranny was festooned with terrifying trim and bizarre baubles.

Amongst them, a giant woolly spider climbing up the side of a three-storeyed pub. But that was not the only creepy-crawly in Whitby for Halloween; it also crawled with tourists. And all of them in their dark and forbidding, sometimes even frightening, steampunk/goth/emo/vampirical finery. But the unexpected storm that hit us on the climactic night of our Whitby visit was more frightening still.

We had huddled together under the vast vault of the cloud-churned sky, barely able to take cover, as the abbey roof had crumbled hundreds of years before that stormy night. Partly from this relentless battering from wind and rain, exposed as it has always been on the head of a cliff looking out to the sombre North Sea. Looming over the town, in one form or another, it has been the most important landmark in this area since the seventh century, acting as a beacon to those traversing these tempestuous waters. What remains today is the hulk of a thirteenth-century monastery, thick with atmosphere and majestic, but not substantial enough to protect the hundreds there that night to celebrate Dracula, Whitby, and good old ghoulish fun. Along with them, we'd signed up for scares, never thinking it would become so real.

Lashed by the unforgiving elements, by a sea and sky apparently enraged by our somewhat surreal celebration, or perhaps out to show us who does it best, we stood there trying to shield our children, all three of whom were with us that night, the canine offspring included, and wondering how the weather forecasters had got it so wrong – 'a little rain might fall' – when a cluster of shrouded figures staggered our way. We shuffled to make room for them, in the spirit of all festivals, when one of them stuck their face in our midst, making all three children scream in unison, loud enough to bring down whatever little roof Whitby Abbey still had. Our gatecrasher's face was not a face at all, but a blank, featureless mass with white pupils to match. He may have been a prankster or a lost soul, looking for a warm spot in a stormy world; either way, it proved too much for our thoroughly sodden kids, already worked up from the spooky atmosphere and spookier storm. Grabbing hold of each, now giggling after the fright, we ran splashing and stumbling through the flooded ruins to our car, a brisk and not-at-all-bracing distance away.

Yet, let me begin at the beginning of how we found ourselves there that fearful night. We had been to Whitby on Halloween as a young couple before, and loved every minute of our romantic rendezvous. Staying at The Moon and Sixpence with an ornate bathtub in the bedroom itself, and the most glorious view of the harbour from our window, we had stirred only to walk around the old town, explore the cobbled lanes and quaint stores, and eat in the fish and chip shops, or the famous herring breakfast or bowl of bouillabaisse in the café under our room. We had strolled along the bracing seafront, and up the storied 199 steps to the abbey, glowing like a guiding light on its headland perch. We had ambled arm in arm along the arcade too, rubbernecking at the hordes in Halloween attire. One sight it had taken my husband a while to tear me away from was the marzipan Dracula in his chocolate coffin, taking up most of a confectioner's shop window. The streetside puppeteer's mournful sea shanty had stopped me in my stride as well. Thoroughly entertained, we had vowed to come back with our children one day. The years passed as we busied ourselves with our two young ones, then we adopted a dog, and it was in the pursuit of the perfect place to holiday with the latter, that a visit to Whitby came up again.

The British love their dogs, and most towns are chock-a-block with them, but a few appear to especially cater to dogs. Whitby with its cheerful dog bakeries and boutiques is one such, and if your pooch likes to swim in the sea and sprint along the shore, if it enjoys the more sedate walks as well, through winding lanes, or bracken and fen to the abbey, sniffing at birds and other dogs (and sometimes Goths and Emos) along the way, then Whitby is the perfect holiday town for it. Many of the holiday cottages too are happy to take dogs. All in all, we couldn't think of a better place for Halloween with the hound than Whitby.

On a crisp October's night, we drove up to Whitby for the weekend. The cottage was down a dark back lane and extremely eccentric inside, with round doors and windows like portholes on a ship. With the strangest looking, even slightly dangerous, revolving stairs that went up a long, thin tower, stopping off at bedrooms along the way. Once the children had chosen their rooms, each with a sea view and a nautical theme, and had their hot chocolate, we retired for the night too, falling asleep relatively quickly from the rigours of the long drive. Till an ear-shattering scream from one of the children's bedrooms woke me with a sickening jolt, sending me hurtling up the revolving stairs, drowsy but determined to go to the rescue of my cubs. Arriving at the first bedroom up the stairs, I found my ten-year-old son screaming his head off and soothed him back into bed, but not before checking the room for intruders. 'What scared you?' I questioned. 'There's a ghost behind the door,' he mumbled drifting off, clearly not terrified enough to stay awake. Behind the door, I found a small white towel puddled on the floor. 'This ghost?' I asked my sleepy son, who appeared to have forgotten that he had ever screamed, bringing his mother sprinting upstairs half asleep. 'It jumped from the door and tried to grab me,' he murmured. 'Really?' I pressed. 'Or did it just flutter to the floor?'

'That last one,' he agreed, before he began to snore. And so, a suitably macabre start was made to our Whitby weekend.

In the morning, with the children having slept better than their rudely awakened parents, we walked into the historic, Halloween-bedecked town. Arriving at the marketplace first, we found it heaving with browsers, buskers, and tradespeople. The latter set out their colourful ware, including jewellery, druidical medicine, and quirky handmade crafts, while the former thronged the tiny cafés, with half an ear on the buskers. In the cobbled lanes that radiate outwards, like a spider's web, were boutiques, delis, curio shops (selling some very curious items indeed), and appropriately monikered pubs and bistros, such as The Witching Post and Rusty Shears, strung up with dancing skeletons and ghostly balloons. Huddled in the centre were the old jewellery shops specializing in the lustrous jet that's picked on the beaches of Whitby, though increasingly hard to find. It became popular in the Victorian era to wear these black stones for mourning, and Queen Victoria herself was seen in jet after Albert's death. At one such shop, amongst the oldest, the man cutting the glistening stone and shaping the silver showed us the pendant he was making of a miniature skeleton hanging from an ivory gibbet, darkly joking with the children about how he'd procured the bone. The dairies with special Halloween 'ice scream' lured us in as well, tempting us into sampling bone-chilling Bramble Stoker in witch's hat cones.

As we walked with our wobbling treats, past the grisly souvenir stalls, to the quiet jetty and beautiful sea views beyond, we were joined by eager Emos, Druids, Dracula fans, and Halloween revellers in costume. With them came a cavalcade of canines, exciting Luna no end. There, with its steampunk owner was a dog in a vampire cape, and just behind us was a five-strong brigade of Brides of Frankenstein who had dressed each of their poodles as Fiona or Shrek. Luna rolled her eyes at their folly, having eschewed almost every Halloween costume we've ever tried to make her wear. With the exception of a flaring lion's mane, which, perhaps because she's rather regal herself, Luna had happily donned to go trick or treating, once as the cowardly lion from *The Wizard of Oz*, and another, as the Gryffindor mascot.

Climbing to the top of one of the two Victorian lighthouses that guard Whitby like sentinels, we scanned the majestic expanse of the cold blue sea for incoming trouble, a storm perhaps, but saw only merry sailboats and the promise of sunshine. A further climb, halfway up the fabled 199 steps, was windswept St Mary's church, and the bench on the bluff by the sea where Dracula had seduced Lucy. As we sat there finishing our ice cream, looking out to distant Norway, we were struck by such a shiver of apprehension that we decided to hurry on. Having booked our places at Whitby Abbey's promised blood-curdling drama that night, the climax of their Halloween celebrations, we saved the climb to the very top for later, working our way back into town instead for our eagerly anticipated fish supper. At The Moon and Sixpence, at which author W. Somerset Maugham is said to have written some of his seminal work, we dug into delicious bowls of steaming gumbo with great gusto. Luna, especially pleased that she'd managed to grab an extra bit of fish from one of her siblings, had a grin on her face that declared, 'All's fair in love and food wars.'

Wandering back to our kooky cottage, we stopped to look at a stately building with a dhoti-clad statue over its door, staring, it would seem, out to sea, like the figureheads on prows of ships. The establishment, we learnt from its plaque, had been a hospital for British Raj marines. More monuments to do with Whitby's seafaring history greeted us on our meander home, from 'Discoverer of Australia' Captain James Cook's statue, to the mammoth, arching whale bones from two centuries ago that frame the best view of the abbey. From the crest on which we stood, we could see past the headland and out to sea, settling on Whitby Abbey over which dusk was falling, and the lights slowly coming on. With festivities on that night, coloured lights swept the abbey grounds, setting its towering stones aglow against the approaching darkness. Like beacons for lost souls.

It had begun to drizzle, despite the early promise of fair weather, and we would have to wrap up, but decided to leave the heavy armoury – long johns and massively padded winter coats – at the cottage. We weren't expecting anything bone-chilling, after all, except the entertainment!

Arriving at the illuminated abbey, we marched through the marshes to its soaring, derelict heart, which was crawling with creepily costumed players, and a nearly-as-scarily togged up audience, most of whom were families like ourselves. Mingling with the spooks, we settled down under a cloud-barred sky to watch the Dracula dramatization for which we'd come all the way from Nottingham. It is not often that one sees a drama played out at the very location in which it was conceived by its creator. So, we were all terribly excited, especially Luna who'd spotted a black cat. It belonged to the witch who kicked off proceedings by singing a dreadful (in more ways than one) ditty. Giggling over it, we were warming up nicely for the evening's grand production, when the loudest crack of thunder we'd ever heard split open the Whitby sky.

The howling wind whipped the rain into an elemental upheaval, turning us from damp and uncomfortable to storm-tossed and distressed within seconds. On a cliff as we were, we could so easily have been blown to our doom had the ancient columns of the abbey not stood between us and the raging sea. Even Luna, at first quite taken with the cat and then the cat's paw weather, had begun to look a bit put out. And as soaked as a drowned kitten. So did we, as did the ghouls huddling in the shadows around us. Some, costumed actors clearly, but others so convincing they could have been real ghosts. Old abbeys, I thought, but didn't say to the children, are bound to house a proper poltergeist or two. Perhaps even a congregation. It was at that moment the masked man jumped into our midst.

Driving back, and diving into our warm beds, after a long day's wanderings (and a hard night's rain), we slept a long, exhausted sleep, glad that no screams in the night or towel ghosts shattered its peace. In the morning, relatively refreshed, we were amazed to see clear blue skies and a peaceful sea stretching before us. Inviting us to one last walk along Whitby beach, with Luna galloping ahead. And so we did, to conclude our (nearly) perfect doggy holiday.

20

Travelling in India
Horn OK Please

The philosophical will tell you that the journey is as important as the destination. This is especially true when you are actually travelling. How smooth your journey, will undoubtedly have a bearing on your holiday mood. How entertaining, how luxurious, or conversely, how bad, will always be seen as a harbinger of things to come. How well you handle the journey is certainly a measure of who you are on holiday. It is, as Rudyard Kipling, the seasoned traveller, said,

> If you can keep your head when all about you
> Are losing theirs...
> If you can wait and not be tired by waiting...
> If you can dream – and not make dreams your master...
> If you can meet with triumph and disaster

And treat those two impostors just the same...
you'll be a Man, my son!

He meant to include women too, I'm sure. But most of all, what he meant to do – clearly – is write the first ever set of survival strategies for travellers, thus laying the ground for all the *Lonely Planets* and *Conde Nasties* that followed. And as a set of travel instructions, they couldn't be more spot-on. To paraphrase that wise man, 'Keep calm, have patience, stay grounded, and carry on!' Because all of this is truer than true when it comes to tripping around India.

Travelling is always eventful in India, because it is Maximum Country. When you throw that many people, with their many languages and cultures and customs and intentions and acts into a single melting pot and expect them to coalesce, you are bound to be disappointed. Or electrified! The sounds *will* overwhelm, the smells assail, the colours dazzle to the point of blinding, and the people pulling every which way bemuse, obstruct, frustrate, and worse. But if you can take it all in your stride and march on (with many deviations) towards your own objectives, you might just have some fun while you're at it! You might find that it is character-building, even life-changing as some travellers attest, sometimes funny, and always, always memorable.

It is probably easiest travelling in India as a young professional whose tickets and transfers have been arranged by someone else (so the hassle is shared; one person organizes and the other executes). Travelling as a parent, a child, an older person, or a young woman without the force-field that business travel can throw around you, can become complicated, or even messy; too often involving harassment, corruption, and sadly, molestation. But if these last three don't happen to you, journeys in India can be enjoyable too. And if you tell me these trips don't make the most entertaining anecdotes afterwards, then you haven't lived (at least not in India).

As a television producer in my mid-twenties, I travelled in and out of Mumbai a lot, and I remember this being silky smooth, even in the early hours, where you could just sashay out with your little suitcase to hail an auto to the airport, and no harm would come to you. But Mumbai airport was good for one more thing, should you be so inclined – star spotting. There always seemed to be 'celebrity log' flying in and out, but one particular occasion proved a windfall. And a mixed blessing.

It would be a middle-of-the-day trip from Kolkata to the Channel [V] offices in Bandra, Mumbai, and back again the following day. Middle-of-the-day wasn't the best time in Mumbai because its many celebrities would have stirred out of bed and been on the move by then, clogging the roads. I preferred travelling in the early hours anyway, with less of my day eaten up in trains and planes. But on this occasion, I was told US President Bill Clinton would be in town too, and he, like me, favoured break-of-day travel. Perhaps he didn't like the glare of a high-noon arrival; maybe he wanted a shadowy entrance because he had something to hide (which, we found later, he did indeed)! Either way, it meant I would have to ride the midday celebrity train to avoid the cordon thrown around him, with its ensuing hold-ups.

Everything ran smoothly on the way in, and after brainstorming work and brain-numbing afterhours 'fun', I was heading back to the airport, confident I'd sidestepped the Clinton convoy. Mumbai's roads are better than Kolkata's, and I was at the airport in a trice. But as I stepped in, I noticed a difference from the previous day; not only was it now packed, there were hundreds of panicky officials running around, getting unnecessarily officious with passengers. Jostled, swept aside, and nearly crushed, unlike any other time on my many television trips there, I couldn't figure out what was happening.

Then it became clear that the crowd was craning to see someone. Had I not managed to evade Clinton after all? Trying to see over the sea of people, even as I was buffeted this way and that, I finally spotted the cynosure of all eyes – and it wasn't Bill! This man had neither the swagger nor the stage presence, and I wondered which Bollywood star could look so unprepossessing and yet create such a stir. But as the thin, balding man approached, weaving through the nonplussed crowd, I was surprised to find quizmaster Siddhartha Basu before me. Was he really the reason behind these huge, surging crowds at Mumbai airport? But the throngs looked as baffled by his appearance as I did, and I pushed on towards my gate.

Yet, the farther I progressed the more congested it got, with hundreds adding to the crush till I was clawing people's backs and fighting for air. At that moment, the crowd started parting like the Red Sea, cheering with the roar of the waves that had crashed upon its shores, and then, in the blinding light at the end of the pathway, I saw GOD. Or, at least, someone close to God for South Asia's millions – Amitabh Bachchan. Though I myself had lost interest in the man, very definitely a man and not a god, at the age of six, his presence explained the frenzied hordes at last. I resigned myself to missing my flight.

In Kolkata though, where anyone can find themselves in the spotlight, the ride can get bumpy very fast. A friend of mine had her own Cinderella story in the then new Kolkata underground, when she, unused to how quickly the subway doors closed (unlike bus doors in the city, which didn't shut at all), left one sandal on the platform as she jumped in. Realizing she'd left it behind but only after the train had started pulling away, she saw a young man pick it up from her window and reconciled herself to its loss. But within minutes the crowd in the carriage had parted to reveal that same young man advancing upon her, holding out her shoe. He had jumped on to a train heading away from his destination just to return her slipper. Prince Charmings obviously did exist!

At other times, however, rides in the wrong direction can send you off the rails. With a day off on Muharram, a university friend and I set out to spend it in the time-honoured manner of devotees everywhere by watching a Hollywood blockbuster. Kevin Costner in *The Bodyguard* at one of the cavernous old cinema halls in central Kolkata to be precise. An event in the city occasioned the complete congestion of already busy roads, and the agitation of its populace, especially if it involved some mass activity like a march, which Muharram did. No agitation, however, could be as great as that of the parents of young Bengali women, who unfailingly provided the latter with a long list of things *not to do* while out and about on such 'dangerous' occasions. Headstrong young women that we were, we were determined to go out, and with little heed to their many instructions on how not to go astray. No crowd, agitation, or upheaval could have stood in the way of our rendezvous with Kevin, our flavour of the month.

It soon became clear we needed a bodyguard more than Whitney when we found ourselves on the wrong side of a seething city. When you're eighteen and excited, you can sometimes mean to board a subway train to central Kolkata and find yourself in its outer reaches. With our whole attention focused on the treat ahead, we neither took notice of the signs on the way to the trains, nor stopped to ask for directions as our parents had instructed. Only when the Kolkata passing our windows turned unusually green, did it strike us we might be heading in the wrong direction. We were a few stops before the southernmost terminus, and running out of time to make our screening. Worse, we kept hearing snatches of conversation about trouble brewing in the central galis of the city.

'There ees hoichoi in Park Circus.'

'Hyan, shunlam. Eet is not cricket.'

'Cricket? Cricket has caused these riots?'

'Pet kharap na matha kharap? Today is Muharram of course.'

'Achcha bujhlam, the Hindu goons and the Muslim goons have attacked each other, making trouble for peaceful people of all religions in our ceety.'

'Bibhotsho! That means the chicken and motton kathi roll shops in that area will have to shut for the day. The best in the ceety! Shorbonash!'

So we panicked and got on the wrong train. It took a while, whispered consultations (we weren't going to give older people the satisfaction of knowing we were abjectly lost), and more running about, before we were on track to commune with Kevin again. When we finally touched down at Esplanade, thanks to our muddled orienteering, we had to run pell-mell on new high heels to get to the old theatre, where we discovered the lobby near-deserted and the ticket counter about to shut. Running into the hall with our hard-won tickets clutched tightly in our fists, we were relieved to discover that though the theatre was dimmed and our seats difficult to find, Kevin himself had yet to make an appearance. If only we had listened to our parents and watched where we were going, we sighed and rolled our eyes, settling down in the cool darkness to forget. And if you asked me now, I wouldn't be able to tell you anything at all about the film, but I remember skipping out of the theatre after the show with a triumphant feeling. Not only had we seen Kevin, we'd heroically accomplished it in the midst of rioting!

Kolkata journeys can be heart-warming too, such as my mellow winter's ride on an ancient Kolkata tram with a Melbourne poet and tram conductor. So enamoured of it was he that he recited Aussie-accented poetry all the way, as kobita-loving bhadralok flocked to him. On that gently sunny December afternoon, our 100-year-old tram merely crawled, sometimes hiccuping a little, as Kolkata went by at a leisurely, after-lunch pace. The decrepit grace of the creeping tram, with the somnolence of the city outside our windows, encapsulated Kolkata better than anything else I could have devised for my guest. Roberto must have thought so too, sending me a lyrical poem he had written about the journey, after his return home.

Journeys home can be as important as those we make to explore the unknown. They say as much about our world and ourselves. Or they can be a pleasant interlude involving biryani. Very pleasant indeed. One branch of my father's family hails from pre-Independence East Bengal, so it is home of sorts but not in any direct or immediate way. Flying into Dhaka in Bangladesh, on my way back to Kolkata from Kathmandu, I was reminded of the times I'd been taunted with being Bangladeshi for my terrible Hindi by Delhi autorickshaw drivers who seemed to think it a particularly offensive insult. At the end of every roughshod ride, I would hand over something approximating the fare and wait for them to return the correct change. They would pretend I didn't exist and look this way and that in an attempt to pocket all the money and not just their due. At which point I would get so exasperated, I would forget what little Hindi I'd learnt, saying as loudly as I could, under the charitable assumption that they were just a little bit deaf rather than thieving whatchamacallits, 'Khuchra hai?' To which they would finally respond, turning towards me with a snarl they appeared to reserve for 'Bangladeshis', 'Bangladeshi hoon?', chucking my change back at me, at the same time, with disdain. And I would be left with no option but to shout after them, as I picked my pennies off the road, in the only language they understood: 'Bangladeshi I may be, but not a bok*ch*** like you!'

In transit in Bangladesh, I expected a similarly disdainful reception at Dhaka airport, this time for not being Bangladeshi enough. Instead, I was greeted with the sweetest smiles and a great deal of interest: 'Bangla bolchen je! Aapni kotha theke?'

'My father's family was from Barisal. My paternal great-grandmother went back regularly even years after Independence.'

'And you? Have you been there?' When I shook my head regretfully, they would launch into lyrical descriptions of its green paddy fields, friendly folk, and delicious fish, till I was convinced that every single customs official at Dhaka airport hailed from Barisal too.

Barisal natives or not, they ensured I was looked after, even well fed, and not just on any old thing, but biryani! It was as delectable as their concern was touching, and if I'd come back from that trip whole, I would have only praise to lavish on my Eastern neighbours. Unpacking on my return, I discovered a side pocket slashed open, and an odd assortment of items, everything I'd shoved in at the last minute, stolen: battery-operated epilator (what, I wondered, did they think it was), nearly finished toothpaste, half-eaten chocolate bar, and the only thing I really regretted losing – an engrossing book I was halfway through.

Airports, more than anything else on a journey, are about ups and downs. At Mumbai airport, once the crowds had moved off with megastar Amitabh Bachchan, I finally found my gate and boarded my flight in the nick of time. Sitting back and closing my eyes for a second, ready to take wing, I heard the captain's public address system crackle to life. 'I'm afraid,' he began and my heart sank, 'that there's a plane just ahead of us waiting to be boarded by a VVIP, and we will have to wait till they're on.' Wait? How much longer? We, passengers, asked the air hostess in unison. But all she had for us was a beatific smile, and a vanishing trick, as she disappeared into thin airplane air. Then we waited and waited, yet again that day, till even exasperation died a death, and giving up on going home for a long while, I joined the other passengers in gaping at the runway and the distant 'special' plane. An hour later, we greeted a silvery head and broad shoulders in the distance with a collective sigh of relief, as well as a spark of curiosity, as a tall man in a suit, with a limber gait, lightly ran up the stairs of the plane ahead of us. After so many near-encounters that day, and despite my many stratagems to avoid him, I had run bang into President Clinton at last. As Monica Lewinsky will avow, some men are impossible to avoid.

21

Hong Kong, Bangkok, and Oman

Schoolgirl Errors

I t's not just India where travel can get complicated.

From as far back as I can remember, it was a frequent feature of our journeys anywhere. I learnt early that travelling with an Indian passport was dicing with danger. It wasn't just the bureaucratic snarls you have to deal with to set foot anywhere, but the ignominy of having to jump through hoops like a circus animal. And all because my passport was the wrong colour (as was I; certainly in the eyes of the world's customs officials). Despite twenty years as a British resident, with an English husband and children, I have hung on to my Indian passport, my Little Blue Book of Horrors. Affectionately named thus, for being the repository for my worst photographs, as well as having, indirectly or otherwise, put me through a hundred harrowing experiences.

Why I've kept it mystifies many. Even me, sometimes. As a joke, I tell people I would fail Norman Tebbit's cricket test if I replaced it with its British counterpart, and I don't like failing. The truth is, I have a complicated love–hate relationship with my passport. I find it hard to let go because this is the identity I came into the world with. It's my umbilical cord with my birth country. But it is also a chain that holds me suffocatingly in place, yanking me back every time I entertain ideas of travelling the world.

We lived in sunny, shiny Southeast Asia in the eighties. We loved it but missed desi food. So after each visit home, we'd cart back a lorry-load of Bong delicacies. Not unexpectedly, we ran into trouble at Southeast Asian airports where Indians were regarded with visceral suspicion. I have often wondered what it was about us, our dress and even our food, that roused such distrust. In Southeast Asia it seemed to stem from their discomfort with Indian emigration to their countries, and even colonization by South Indian kings in the dim and distant past. In the Philippines, this deep-seated dislike found its way into kids' nightmares in the shape of a bogeyman their parents called 'The Bumbayia', The Man from Bombay, a turbaned shadow that snatched children from their beds.

One year, we were transporting the hugest, hardest slab of sludge-brown palm sugar when we were stopped at Bangkok airport. Bangkok was bad luck for us, but this colourful city with its delectable delicacies, tooting tuktuks, grand palace with arresting stone monsters, golden Buddhist temples, with Buddha himself in distinctive poses in each, always drew us back. My favourite pagoda was the one in which Buddha reclined with such serenity, that Chilled Buddha was how I thought of him. Chilled would *not* be how I'd describe Bangkok's customs officials though. 'What's this?' they glared as we filed past them. 'Jaggery,' we replied. 'Gargari?' they gurgled in alarm, pulling on latex gloves and poking it vigorously. When nothing happened, they edged closer to detect coughs, rattles, or ticking. Unconvinced by its listlessness, they decided to split it open. But jaggery, as any Indian worth his sugar knows, is one tough cookie. When their attempts at penknife-dissection failed, out came curmudgeonly cleavers with which they hacked it into a gargantuan, gooey mess. Still nothing. As they cast around for their next move, my howling baby sister took matters into her own hands, or mouth should I say, throwing up explosively over the cane-sugar carnage, and – to our barely concealed delight – the officials. They couldn't get rid of us quick enough.

Hong Kong too was a rocky ride from the get-go. At three hours, the flight from Manila was not nearly as long as the one that took us to Kolkata to visit family while we lived in the Philippines. We were older too than the first time we had made that sea crossing from old home to new, and known that first heart-flutter of embarking on an adventure, balanced by the wrench of leaving, as we watched Kolkata fade away. But then, the amazing cloud formations, the blonde, doll-like SAS air hostesses, the likes of whom I'd never seen before, and the food – miniature dinners full of alien flavours that barely tasted of anything – tickled, if not my taste buds, brought up on the full flavours of India, then my fancy at least.

We were battle-scarred veterans of nine and three by the time we got to Hong Kong, after years of face-offs with airport officials, and misadventures in the air. So this hop-over to another South China Sea island wasn't expected to be any more turbulent than our usual trips. But just as a very smooth flight was coming to an expected smooth end, the pilot announced that weather conditions had changed in the course of the flight, in the flash that it often did in these parts. Amidst an eruption of rain and winds in previously unruffled skies, landing on the runway was going to be a little more 'exciting' than anticipated. Even as the pilot announced this, a judder ran through the metallic body of the plane, and the faint titters with which the pilot's attempt at humour had been received, turned into a collective groan. Air travel was still new to many people.

Kai Tak, Hong Kong's airport at the time, was like few in the world. Designed, as it seemed to be, for cinematic exploits rather than safe travel, it stood in the centre of Kowloon with its airstrip extending into the sea. As a result, flying into Hong Kong could be exhilarating, hemmed in by sea, skies, and skyscrapers, but it could be unnerving too. Not only was it a sea landing, there was a hill in the way, so some nifty, airy calisthenics were required to land, including a 45-degree spin to align with the airstrip, and a stretch in the air under 500 feet, weaving between the multi-storeys. In the rain, the runway often disappeared as well. This made for great filmy stunts with an appropriately breathtaking backdrop, but when it's being executed by the plane you're in, finding it more harrowing than fun is likely.

On that bright summer's day that had darkened in the blink of an eye, with the plane wobbling ever so often, the passengers sat in breathless silence inside it. Would it drop like a pin from the sky? Would it sink in the fathomless sea? Then the plane swooped unexpectedly, and someone let out a shriek. From our windows, we could plainly see it was within a hair's breadth of the sea. We felt its exertions too, rocking like a buoy in the deep. Then it lifted itself slightly, enough to inch over the runway instead of plunging beneath. The big wheels touched down with a shudder, and as the plane roared down the runway, the tannoy came alive with the announcement we had all hoped to hear: 'We have arrived in Hong Kong.'

As our taxi careened through the narrow streets, with stalls along the sidewalks and low-hanging laundry overhead, we spied people at every window. They hung about on the streets too, slurping bowls of steaming noodles, whilst others rushed busily back and forth. This absorbing drama unfolded across a landscape of bendy (built to withstand frequent earthquakes) towers, floods of traffic, and illuminated jumbles of store fronts and shop signs, half-obscured by the vapour from washing and dimsum. That impression of everything stacked on top of each other in Hong Kong was in keeping with its aspirational outlook. I could have spent all week watching its hurly burly, but we had plans to partake of it too.

At the sailing junk market at the harbour, threading in and out of the crowds of cyclists, vendors, and hagglers on the pier, we watched the trading boats bob closer, whilst the junks sailed out with their golden dragons on scarlet sails unfurled. The scent of Chinese food cooking on the market boats drew us in several mouth-watering directions at the same time, ultimately taking us to the waterborne stall from which wafted the most alluring fragrance of wok-tossed prawns in sticky ginger sauce. We didn't just love food, especially Chinese food, we enjoyed a spectacle too, and the stallholder on this bright blue boat was putting on quite a show. Leaping every time the crackling oil made the prawns jump out of the wok, he sang and cracked jokes for his customers crowding round. We couldn't understand a word of it but his toothy smile made us laugh. Tucking into our little tubs of crustacean delights, then saying yes to a second when it arrived, I felt at peace with the world that sunny mid-morning in Hong Kong.

As I swept the last morsel into my snaggle-toothed, nine-year-old mouth, a long, gleaming car swept up to our sated huddle, and a long, gleaming Chinese driver stepped out. It turned out that my father, feeling quite unlike himself, had hired us a car for that afternoon. We had places to go and things to see. As the car took to the narrow congested streets, a feeling overtook me that was both familiar and not, threatening to spill over. Was it the pleasure of being in a wondrous new place? Was it excitement at the thought of everything we were planning to do that day? Or could it be a little-girl crush on the handsome Keanu Reeves lookalike at the wheel?

When the car lurched to a stop at our first port of call, a museum of fine arts, an oasis of calm and sophistication, I found out what it was that was swelling inside me. Not excitement, not feverish delight, not even a crush. Instead, it was our family's dreaded curse, that secret scourge which visited us at the least opportune moments. The unhappy recipient of this particular family gene for those years of my childhood when we were almost constantly on the road, I saw the driver's slick-as-a-seal head nodding to us with just a hint of a handsome smile in his mirror, and recognized the sensation that had overtaken me. And that I couldn't hold it in any more. Like a fountain it arced from my seat to his. Puke of such precision, it spattered nothing at all, leaving me and the car sparkly clean, filtering accurately into the space between his starched collar and gleaming neck, to slide down the back of his pristine suit, as we all watched in horror. But he didn't bat an eyelid, change expression, swear, or reprimand, getting stiffly out of the car to hold the door open, impervious to our many apologies. But he did break the family jinx, because I never threw up again. Anywhere. And I thought I was rid of it forever till my children started leaning over in cars to fetch back, not just their breakfasts but the family curse.

The family blight may not be motion sickness though, but attracting trouble on our travels because that certainly did not end in childhood. Two decades later, I found myself alone in Oman for a few hours. After a lifetime of trouble in transit, I decided to steer clear of anything that might land me in it, and sit quietly at the airport. Having cleared security without any hassle, I planted my rear firmly in a seat by the departure gate and my nose in a book: *The Luck of the Bodkins*. I tried even to ignore the call of nature but eventually concluded I could risk a little trip to the loo. What disaster could possibly befall me there? There was nothing major I needed to do. I'd be in and out in a jiffy.

That's when I realized that disaster could indeed follow me *anywhere* because, despite latching and unlatching from my side several times, I could not open my cubicle door. Embarrassed though I felt to make a racket, I pushed and pulled with all my might, rattling it about to see if it would budge. But it didn't. Then, more disconcertingly still, it dawned on me that I would have to call out. So, I cleared my throat and yelped, 'Help.' No response. I raised my voice a tad to venture, 'Help, my door's jammed.' Still nothing. Finally, with a sigh, knowing that a scene was unavoidable, I hollered for all I was worth, banging on the unyielding door at the same time. I could still hear no one at all on the other side of the door. When, with a totally unexpected whoosh, like a dark cloud descending from the dim ceiling, a fast-moving robed figure jumped into the cubicle with me. With a flurry of flying limbs, they delivered a smooth but brutal kick to the door, which, groaning like a felled tree, swung back to set me free. This blur of black robes and martial arts moves, who was a Ninja surely (I thought, too dumbstruck to say it aloud), turned to me with eyes that laughed from behind her burka, to ask in a young woman's voice, 'Are you all right? I am airport security.'

Although it proved that there wasn't anywhere in the world where trouble won't follow me, it also showed me that occasionally, just very occasionally, airport officials can be helpful too, though rarely with as much pizzazz.

Pause for Thought: Gallivanting with a Gaggle

Travelling with loved ones, or a nucleus of like-minded people, is generally smoother than going on an excursion with a whole gaggle of friends or co-workers who push and pull in different directions. Noise, when travelling with a large group, is almost unavoidable. But you might be off on a huge shindig – for New Year's Eve or a bachelor's party – and noise is exactly what's desired. Or it could be a work junket where the hundreds of ideas bouncing off each other is precisely what it needs. But if it's a more relaxed holiday you want, or to work in a quiet, contemplative environment, then large numbers are a no-no.

Even work outings can be pared down to the minimum and function better that way. Such as the time I went to shoot a story on Mayapur, the ISKCON stronghold in Bengal, with just my cameraman for company rather than the whole crew (always comprising a few whose roles nobody really knew). On the face of it, Mayapur was a complex of serene marble temples and harmonious communes. Yet, it was not to breathe in the spirituality of this setting that we needed a trip without clamour, but to hear beyond what our interviewees were saying, to the stories that lay beneath, in that controversial place.

It isn't just about numbers either, but who makes them up. You could go on holiday craving quiet, with a bosom buddy or two, and find yourself dragged to nightclubs or roped in for a singalong show. But you could as easily travel with a large contingent and still snatch relaxed interludes: either because they leave you to your pleasures, or want the same gentle delights as you. Alternatively, a knees-up could be just what the doctor ordered, but meditation and spa treatments are what you get, because you fell in with your tripmates.

Your fellow travellers, I've said before but can't say enough, are key. Yes, even more than your meticulously researched vacation spot. Though hitting upon the right number touring with you is crucial too, and how many different sources of fun but also strain you can tolerate is ultimately about individual bandwidth. For me, more than six people is too many, but for some that might be sixteen or twenty-six.

So, when you're planning your trip, try this mental exercise of slotting your friends. Is he perhaps a Joey from the American sitcom *Friends*, keen to play a boisterous game of Fireball in your shared hotel bedroom in the day, and sneak 'chicks' in at night? But he'll also cheerfully cover for you, taking the fall himself, if *you* get caught doing the above. He could also be a Ross: perfectly capable of being annoying but in a quieter way, and as good a friend in need, but happier to do his bit from behind the scenes. Monica will keep you clean and well-fed, but be a pain about holiday rules, and Phoebe will comfort you with made-up songs, yet flake when practical skills are required. They can all in their own way make splendid tripfellas; so choose wisely and you can't go wrong.

But remember, how well your friends gel on your wander is essential to good holiday vibes. Chucking Chandler, Fonzi, and *Big Bang*'s Sheldon together won't make for happy days!

If, despite choosing your tripchums sagely, the number accurately, and ensuring they all get along, you still get disharmony on holiday, keep those books handy, good music on tap, and a water-colour set. A reasonable camera and a few jaunts planned just for yourself make for the perfect safety net. Most of all, keep some cash spare – you never know when you might need a quick, quiet exit.

22

Nainital

The One with Friends

'I shared a bed with a pair of twins,' I sometimes say if conversation is beginning to flag. At other times, I've been known to reminisce, 'When I worked at Sonagachhi, Kolkata's red light district...' Both have the desired effect of stopping the person I'm speaking to in their tracks, allowing me to steer the conversation away from the trivialities they're trundling on with. Neither is true of course, or at least, only partly. I have never been a sex worker, though I did do a series of stories on AIDS for MTV News that took me places 'good' girls don't usually go. I've also never had sex with a pair of twins. And so I usually explain those initial pronouncements, once the person's jaw has touched the floor, and they've ceased droning about inanities, especially if they are of an advanced age and infirmities. Not wanting the responsibility for some elderly relative dropping from apoplexy, I make it perfectly clear that I've never had sex for money, or with twins, but that I did share a bed with a pair on holiday. Because there were more friends on that trip than beds.

Young, impulsive, and tired of the daily grind of television reporting, we yearned for a change of scene (though how fortunate were we, I think in retrospect, to be in that position fresh out of university). So, on the spur of the moment, with no warning, no research, and most of all, no room bookings, we decided to head for the hills. To spend the weekend in Nainital in the Himalayan foothills. The drive up from Delhi in the weeny car of a friend who had just learnt to drive was eventful to say the least, compounded by there being far too many in it. Squished together, on top, or underneath, we started out on Friday night to get there the next morning. Stopping liberally along the way for parathas and chai at rickety roadside stalls, or to answer nature's call, or even for itchy body parts that couldn't be reached in the crush. We all had to pour out each time, cramming ourselves in again when the itch (both literal and figurative) had been scratched. Amidst all this, there was naturally no chance to make bookings (and back in the day anyway we had neither mobiles nor apps).

It was only when we got there on a crisp Saturday morning, disgorging from the car in front of a row of modest chalet-style hotels, that it struck us we had nowhere to place our luggage, and more importantly, our heads for the night. But young people are optimistic, so with light hearts and broad smiles, we marched into the first hotel and asked for rooms. This carried on for several hotels, with steadily diminishing smiles and worse, chances of finding rooms, till we came to the shabbiest, and from the frown on the receptionist's face, most unwelcoming. The eleven of us needed a handful of rooms at least, so the reluctant male receptionist called the manager over from his armchair in the corner to confer, and they both glared at us together. We looked like a motley crew.

The twins, who would blossom into TV stars a decade later, were long, stick thin, and identically dressed in lumber jackets. The other six boys were a strange range of shapes, sizes, facial hair, and sartorial elegance (or the lack thereof). One of them, a gentle soul really, was a hulking lad with a buzz cut and mad glint in his eye. The women with me, on the other hand, were nicely turned out, whilst I was in my regulation blue jeans and tee. After a long scrutiny, the hotel management conceded they could stretch to four rooms. The beds were HUGE, they assured us. 'Three rooms for the boys and one for the girls,' the receptionist decided on our behalf. With three women and eight men, this arrangement might have worked (though my personal bubble didn't care for intrusions from any gender), had it not been for the two pairs of lovebirds who had other ideas. They'd got away from their homes in Delhi for some 'couples time' and were not going to have our comfort stand in their way. As the only girl in the group who was not part of a couple, it fell upon me to share my room with some of the young men. I murmured that I didn't know them that well. Not yet. Nor had any such plans.

My youthful friends were in no mood to sit and mull over sleeping arrangements however, so off we went into the quaint old town that hugs the verdant hills. Nainital, like many other

Himalayan resorts, was once a summer retreat for the British in India. A site of legends, its famous eye-shaped lake had been a lure for pilgrims for much longer than that. But it was the British that built a small conurbation around it in 1841, because it had the green vistas and pleasant climate they so loved. In these colonial towns of the Himalayan foothills, the sun did shine but was never too hot. At its most dazzling, it turned the skies a brilliant blue and the hills a golden green, but the rest of the time, it drizzled just like the English adored. It reminded them of home.

When we visited more than a century-and-a-half later, vestiges of its past remained in the shabby colonial buildings, including our hotel with its hanging eaves, wrought-iron balustrades, and rickety four-poster beds. It echoed in the winding lanes, ornate lakeside arcades, and blooming bandstands. As we meandered through Nainital's serpentine streets, breathing in the fresh mountain air (especially fresh after smoggy Delhi), we each spotted attractions that lured us away from the group. The single men were lost to a gaming arcade into which they were lured by the more modern charms of Donkey Kong and the Mario Brothers. The couples parked themselves on benches, in flowering pavilions, and eventually on boats, simpering at each other. I had to choose a squad to stick to, and plumped for watery wanderings over video game violence, but kept my distance and my own counsel (aka, clung to the side of the boat and talked to myself).

As the boat ride dragged, and I tired of the constant cooing in my ear, I spotted something that interested me far more. A restaurant. Not a roadside stall, nor even the standard

North Indian eatery which was all I had access to in Delhi
(a range of droolsome restaurants existed, but they were rarely
cheap, unlike in my hometown of Kolkata), this one was a
proper continental bistro, with a striped awning over the door
and a maître d' under it. There were posies and twinkling
lamps at each table, coming on one by one as the sun dipped
behind the lake. The restaurant, situated on a pier, appeared
to float on the tarn, and so close that when I leaned out of
the boat, not only could I see its sign – a curlicued 'Paris to
Pompeii' – but its exotic menu! As I read through it quickly
(before our boat moved on), my mouth watered at the pâtés
and parfaits, the coq au vin and crabcakes, the taramasalatas
and tiramisus. I had spent many a Delhi night dreaming of
such dinners, oozing with wine and cream and cocoa, before
downing my daily dal and falling asleep. To dream again of a
smorgasbord of delights. But this time it was real and within
reach! I had quickly checked the prices and, amazingly, it
wasn't beyond our means. I could almost taste it.

I turned around to tell my boatmates I had found the
perfect restaurant for the night. Here, in a British Raj town in
the hills, was the chance to eat something different. Goulash
perhaps or shepherd's pie. With apple crumble and clotted
cream to round it off. My eyes shone, and I babbled from
the excitement. But they weren't listening. 'Your tiny pursed
mouth, how I long to hear you sing from it,' said one to the
other, and their lover replied, 'Oh, I will. I will coo to you
like a kabuttar, because don't you look just like Salman Khan
in *Maine Pyar Kiya*!' I steeled myself not to throw up; it would
never do, not with such a gorgeous dinner waiting. When we

returned to shore to join the gamers, finally able to break my exciting news to them, I waited for them to jump with joy and thank me profusely for spotting the place. Instead, they turned to each other and said, '*Kya chahiye tujhe? Roti-sabzi hai na?*'

No one else was interested in the lakeside restaurant with the old-world charm. None of them wanted to sip wine as they watched the water rippling on the lake. Or tuck into a comforting Confit while contemplating the gilding of the hills by the departing sun. Or have a quiet conversation for a change, without having to raise our voices over the honking horns, the blaring loudspeakers, the people haggling at the stalls that dotted every lane. Don't get me wrong; much good grub's to be had at such places around India, and the colour and noise can be energizing. But sometimes, just sometimes, I wanted something different. Living in England now, we cook lots of Indian food because wherever in the world I am, I enjoy variety. If variety is the spice of life, let us ensure we sprinkle the last liberally with panch phoron, ajinomoto, as well as rosemary and thyme. And Nainital, a town of two halves, the shabby grace of what it once was, quietly fronting the colour and squalor of what it had become, afforded the opportunity to dip into both.

The truth of travelling with a gaggle is that no matter how fond you are of them, it's not pleasant to have to constantly subsume your interests to those of others. In theory, it's a barrel of fun – all those different personalities in the mix, making the trip livelier than it would be with your family or like-minded partner. But in fact, it rarely works that way. Like a sack of skirmishing kittens, it goes from being adorable and entertaining to unmanageable and annoying very quickly. Nowhere more so than in the areas of what to visit and where to dine. It was quite possibly the experience that followed that put me off travelling with friends forever after. It was proof that no matter how well you get along, or how much they make you laugh, if they are not in tune with you, it will involve far too many sacrifices and false diplomacies. I've been on plenty of day trips with a mixed bunch of friends since then and enjoyed them thoroughly, but have attempted (with some success) to dodge the longer, more likely to be grating, durations away. And though the 'friends' holiday might feel like a social imperative and a measure of your popularity, it's quite all right to let yourself off that hook if you don't enjoy it.

This lesson of listening to your inner voice, or in this case, tummy, I learnt particularly well in Nainital. In the spirit of bonhomie, I went along with their choice of roadside stall for the night, gulping down roti and sabzi by the side of a cacophonous road where jostling elbows vied for space with cycles, stray dogs, and a spectrum of goods for sale. Everyone had something to say and everyone else wanted right of way. Nor was there anything at all wrong with what we ate, or rather, if there was something wrong, which subsequent events proved, it was not its taste. It filled my stomach sure enough, but then it upset it. It doesn't take a lot to upset my delicate Bengali constitution. Anything that is heavy on spices and light on hygiene (sadly true of some roadside food) will send alarm bells ringing through my innards. This particular meal didn't just ring alarm bells, but set the Big Ben of all gastric upheavals roiling. I was off like a shot down the road, off like my friends every time I wanted to step back and savour the setting. This time, it was I who had no time, as W.H. Davies would've said, to 'stand and stare' because I needed to get to our hotel quick. Superquick. As I ran I saw them over my shoulder, bewildered and then aghast at my sudden and fleet-footed retreat. I was not allowed to forget it either, nor did I my resolve to never go on holiday with them or any other gaggle again!

With my stomach heaving and head spinning, I had to lie down as soon I got back to our hotel room. It was then that I realized how narrow the bed was. It looked imposing from the outside, with its four carved wood posts and draped net, but it was titchy within. And I was going to have to share this with not one but two men double my size? Anxiously mulling it over as the room spun around me, I fell asleep. When I awoke with the insistent feeling that I'd have to dash to the antiquated loo again, there were two large bodies on either side of me, snoring heavily. Scrambling over their never-ending legs I got there in time, but when I returned shaking and weak, they were both up and staring at me. I groaned inwardly. Maybe outwardly as well. The last thing I needed was two young men watching my drama of heaving, trembling, and puking, keenly. Nice looking ones they were too, I thought distantly, but what good is that when you need kindness and comfort?

Then, one of them said, taking me utterly by surprise, 'I know what you need because my mother makes it for me when I'm sick. I will get you some hot water, honey, and lemon from the kitchen.' And off he scooted. 'Let me help you back into bed,' said the other, vacating it himself. 'Would you like a second blanket? You are shivering. Why not have mine?'

When the first one returned with the concoction and medicine he'd managed to get from the hotel kitchen, in my woozy state, I'd forgotten they were twins and thought I was seeing double. The one who'd remained with me propped me up for my drink, but it was something else I needed to do. As I got up unsteadily to go, the face of the one with the drink scrunched up in concern, as the other suddenly dived for the floor to catch a falling vase, or something equally precious. I have no further recollections of that night, but if I got through it, it was in no small measure due to my identical male nurses. Nothing exciting happened, it's true, but you could argue that spilling your guts on someone is intimacy too.

I woke the next morning feeling so much better that the apple-pie-and-ice-cream cravings returned. The dissolution of the stars of disorientation that had danced through my night of illness left that little continental restaurant's menu floating tantalizingly before me instead, especially the description of their walnut brownie sundae. It convinced me that a long, cool glass of creamy indulgence, the chocolate sauce streaming from the top to settle in a yummy puddle at the base, and the crunchy, bittersweet tang of the nuts sprinkled over the top could be my 'hair of the dog', or the food to cure the ills that food had brought the night before. Furthermore, I resolved, it was my duty, not only to myself, but to generations of future travellers in a quandary about what to follow: their friends or their heart, to rectify the wrongs of the day before, and strike out on my own.

With just over an hour left before we piled back into the teeny car to head back to the heat, dust, and dal-chawal of Delhi, I marched out to have that much-desired meal with what money I had left. I did ask my night-time nurses to join me so I could thank them fittingly, but they rolled their eyes at my gluttony even as they gave me their blessings. Donkey Kong called and they would not be joining me, but they promised not to leave me behind. Clutching my hard-earned TV trainee money, I went back to the beautiful café by the lake. I was looking forward not just to the food but the solitude, never having eaten at a restaurant alone before. As I approached it, the awning fluttered in welcome, while the burnished sign shimmered in the sun, and the beaming man at the door ushered me in. 'Table for one!' I declared with a confidence I wouldn't have ordinarily felt, but there was something charmed about the place. It seemed to exist only for me. Escorted to a table by a big glass window overlooking the fluid greys and greens of the lake, I felt a similar shift within me. I was ready to start doing things my way.

Sinking into the shabby chintz of my chair, I breathed in the fragrance of the Himalayan meadow flowers on my table, and even headier scents of the food in the establishment. I didn't have to look at the menu; I remembered it well from the day before. 'I would have a gazpacho for starters, and seafood risotto for mains...' I smiled at the man scribbling it all down, finishing with the tiramisu I'd dreamt of for a year. I would savour them alongside the views of soaring hills and sparkling waters. And so I did, achieving an afterglow no romp with twins could provide!

But then with a jolt I observed the time, and like a fairy-tale princess about to mutate into a pumpkin, I tore myself away from my Prince Charming of a luncheon with a view, my perfect afternoon alone, to hotfoot it back to our car parked in front of the hotel and ready to go. Back in the nick of time and out of breath, I realized how much of a Cinderella story it had proved, because I'd left my scarf behind at the restaurant. I never got it back but that was okay, because I'd discovered something else – how to be my own woman.

With a little help from my friends.

23

London

Orf with Their 'Eads

'Rain, rain, go away,' I breathed as I stepped out into a wet London morning. The kind of morning I prefer to stay indoors, wrapped in a pashmina and nursing a cup of hot lemony tea, watching the world get very wet. That was not to be on that late summer morning, because I had guests from India eager to explore London. But they had visited the Big Smoke before and taken in most of the sights, so my challenge was to show them aspects of this city that were (to them) utterly new. My friends and I shared a passion for architecture and strangely, nursery rhymes. We had always found the history behind the seemingly innocuous English ditties we grew up with intriguing. I decided to combine these interests to create a new way of seeing London. With a little research, I found the landmarks with the most enthralling, grisly, as well as the funniest links to the hoariest rhymes. With every inch of London boasting literary or historic connections, it was the perfect city for such a tour.

Catching a red double-decker bus to The Eagle, a pub in Shoreditch, where I'd arranged to meet my friends, I was pleasantly surprised to find the skies clearing. As we fortified ourselves for the three-hour walk with hearty portions of mustard-spiked mash topped with coils of pork and leek bangers, I announced to their surprise, 'Our tour begins right here.'

The roundel referring to this historic public house located at the corner of Shepherdess Walk and City Road runs:

> Up and down the city road,
> In and out the Eagle.
> That's the way the money goes,
> Pop! goes the weasel...

Starting life as a pub, The Eagle did a turn as a music hall in the early nineteenth century, returning as a pub after being demolished in 1901. A plaque at the door reminds visitors of its connection with the rhyme. The ditty uses cockney rhyming slang in a coded message about hard times – 'weasel' is short for 'weasel and stoat' which means coat. And 'pop' was a colloquial term for pawning, harking back to the dire poverty of Victorian London's underbelly, where a coat would often have to be traded for a crust of bread. The verse mentioning this pub was first heard during a performance at the Theatre Royal in 1856.

The Eagle was just shabby enough to evoke nostalgia for the era in which it was immortalized. The brooding air created by the dark walls and a soaring iron eagle atop its central dome was a reminder of the uncomfortable Victorian juxtaposition of grandeur and despair that nineteenth-century London was famous for.

Our next stop was linked to perhaps the most London-centric of all nursery rhymes. 'Oranges and lemons, say the bells of St Clement's,' I hummed under my breath as we walked,

> You owe me five farthings,
> Say the bells of St Martin's.
> When will you pay me?
> Say the bells of Old Bailey.
> When I grow rich,
> Say the bells of Shoreditch…

I stopped as we came upon St Leonard's in Shoreditch, fifteen minutes from The Eagle. With time for only brief halts at each of the many churches in this fruity but macabre ballad about death and taxation, ache as we might to step into the calm of grand St Leonard's, we had to push on through the hurly-burly of London streets to the Theatre Royal in Drury Lane, Covent Garden.

A succession of buildings at this location since 1663 has made this the oldest working theatre in London. The leading playhouse until it caught fire in 1672, a larger, Christopher Wren creation rose from its ashes two years later. The one we stood in now, from 1812, had seen the likes of Ivor Novello, Monty Python, and the stellar casts of Andrew Lloyd Webber musicals on its stage. And though we felt a shiver of apprehension that the masked Phantom may step out from behind a sumptuous velvet curtain to sing, to us it was this theatre's links with not just one – 'Pop Goes the Weasel' – but *two* historic rhymes that made it special.

> Do you know the muffin man,
> The muffin man, the muffin man?
> Do you know the muffin man,
> Who lives in Drury Lane?

I recited to my friends as they shook their heads grinning. In the Victorian age, when muffins were delivered door-to-door, many would have been brought to the players who staged more shows in a day than they do today. The theatre itself would not have been the richly restored, four-tiered, 2,000-seat extravaganza it is now. The detailed restoration had returned its finest features – the rotunda, royal staircases, and grand saloon – to their former Regency glory. It left us salivating but that could have been caused by the mention of muffins.

On the forty-minute walk through Fleet Street to London Bridge, our next destination, were two more 'Oranges and Lemons' churches. St Sepulchre at Old Bailey was more impressive than we expected, being the largest parish church in London. Music filled the aisles as we wandered in for a look at Pocahontas's lost love John Smith's resting place.

> When will that be?
> Say the bells of Stepney.
> I do not know,
> Says the great bell of Bow...

Rang the tune in our ears as we arrived at St Mary-le-Bow located in the shadow of the magnificent St Paul's. This imposing old city church is vested with great meaning for the cockneys of London. Tradition has it, only those born within earshot of the bells of Bow are true cockneys. As the bells began ringing, our stomachs rumbled, and we made our way to a Thames-side bench to feast on a large bag of roasted chestnuts bought from a vendor. London Bridge loomed before us. As we sat watching it shimmer in the early afternoon haze, a street performer crept up to us, and with a knowing twinkle in his eye sang,

> London Bridge is falling down,
> Falling down, falling down.
> London Bridge is falling down,
> My fair ladeeez.

The story goes that when King Henry III put the taxes from the bridge at Queen Eleanor's disposal in 1269, she blew it all on a thirteenth-century version of retail therapy. As a result, the bridge fell into serious disrepair. In the winter of 1281, frost wreaked havoc on the shaky structure, and a section fell into the river. The song was then sung from one end of London to the other in angry criticism of the Queen.

In reality, London Bridge is not one but several historical bridges that traversed the Thames between the old City of London and Southwark in central London over the centuries. Its latest incarnation is a steel-and-concrete structure, but it had humble beginnings as a timber bridge built by London's Roman founders. Similar short-lived crossings followed, eventually supplanted by a sturdy medieval construct that survived 600 years before its replacement in the nineteenth century with an arched stone bridge. Though each of them fell down, as London's only crossing across the Thames till the mid-eighteenth century, London Bridge had to be resurrected time and again.

Leaving the bridge, we walked north, pausing at St Martin's and St Clement's of 'Oranges and Lemons' fame just long enough to take in their soaring spires and snippets of history. All that remained of the first was its bell tower, while the second, located on the wharves, still smelled of the citrus fruit seamen unpacked on its doorstep. We couldn't help but wonder why these beautiful churches had been drafted into that macabre old dirge about child sacrifice, public executions, and the deadly marital troubles of Henry VIII.

Thinking uncharitable thoughts of Henry, its most famous incumbent, we headed east along Eastcheap and entered the imposing and still somewhat forbidding Tower of London, now a museum, treasury, and UNESCO World Heritage Site. This complex of moated, fortified castles is spread over eighteen acres. In its heyday, it was both a palace and a prison, as well as the stronghold the English royalty retreated to under siege. Thus the castle's connection with the ditty 'Mary, Mary, Quite Contrary', a rhyme about Henry VIII's daughter Mary I, who took refuge in the Tower when England rose up against her misrule and mass executions.

Mary, Mary, quite contrary,
How does your garden grow?
With silver bells and cockle shells,
And pretty maids all in a row.

That's not all. 'Oranges and Lemons', with its grisly last line on decapitations, and 'Pop Goes the Weasel', which is often interpreted as mockery of Henry's weakness for bumping off wives, are also linked to the Tower of London. Seen as a place of dark deeds like torture, murder, and beheadings, the castle gets its name from the iconic White Tower within it, which was the earliest stone keep in England.

Sixteenth-century zealots and nineteenth-century literati colluded over the ages to give the Tower its sinister reputation. A good many people were indeed executed on the grounds, but only seven were killed inside the tower complex. Two were Henry's wives and another two, both women, were put to death on his express orders. Anne Boleyn, the first of his wives slain here, is said to haunt it still, wandering its corridors with her severed head tucked under her arm. As we stood on the exact spot where she had breathed her last, hoping to catch sight of her ghost to round off an entertaining tour, the heavens opened up again.

Dashing out of the complex, wet but excitedly recounting the high points of our rhyming tour, we were stopped by an American couple looking for pointers and tips. I handed them my tour plan as we rushed to catch a red double-decker headed our way. 'How was it?' I heard them yell at our retreating backs. 'Brilliant,' my friends threw over their shoulders as they ran. 'We'd do it again!'

24

Nepal

The Hills Are Alive

Standing in the lobby of the Taj Bengal in Kolkata was Oscar-winning Ismail Merchant of Merchant Ivory, sweating in his Hawaiian shirt despite the powerful air-conditioning of the opulent hotel. I was on time but he was already waiting, radiating an energy to equal the noontime sun. But he was gentle too, greeting me softly when I expected him to bellow. It was the 1st of December and World AIDS Day in that penultimate year of the previous millennium, and he had agreed to speak about his experiences of losing friends and colleagues to the illness within the moviemaking fraternity.

Though young, it was not my first story on the disease that had devastated the last decades of the twentieth century. Nor was I new to television journalism, having worked with international channels since finishing university, and in the fortunate position of being regional head of a multinational music channel in my mid-twenties. But I had begun to chafe at the lack of 'real' stories that came my way, and 'real' people that I could connect to at a deeper level.

With me that afternoon, and indeed a lot of the time those days, was Thom, our gangling, beringed researcher, Amal, our grinning (but actually shy, it turned out) VJ, and our camera and sound crew of Gopal and Ganesh, who behaved like twins but were twenty years and kilograms apart. Plus, wherever cameras went in India, hangers-on would materialize, and this was no exception. As the cameras rolled and I established the tilt and tempo of our chat, with our VJ standing by to top and tail the segment, Ismail settled into comfortably expansive stories of both his films and the AIDS crisis.

One of the stories he told us was of an ailing friend on a mission to climb Mt Everest, whose journey to Nepal had not ended with the successful summit attempt he'd planned, but with determination, drawn from the people and the mountains, to fight the disease. 'He said to himself then,' related Ismail with drama and real feeling, '"I have got more from this trip than I could have hoped for – a new family of fellow sufferers and supporters – and I didn't even get past the boulders at the base of Everest. But it was worth every minute."' As Thom shed a tear and Amal cleared his throat of a sob, I knew we must follow that story to Nepal.

In Manipur earlier that year to report on a big rock concert featuring some of India's best known bands, we had spent as much time disappearing down rabbit holes to unknown neighbourhoods and hidden communities as covering the glitz and clamour of the music festival. Speaking to young men and women, doctors and activists, in decrepit districts neglected by both the local and national government, we knew we'd found stories that needed to be told. Of drug addiction and AIDS infections, contracted from sharing needles, taking over the lives of youngsters in the forlorn towns near the Sino-Indian border. Yet, the courage of these charming, forgotten people, coping with curfews and little economic support, gave us as much hope as the concert coming to town.

Nepal, which we travelled to a few months later, was rocking too at the turn of the millennium. Before it was shaken in a whole different way by the assassinations of the Nepalese King Birendra and his family. But that was months away when we travelled to crisply sunny Kathmandu, as it readied to roll in the new millennium, and though we had serious stories planned, we had every intention of soaking up those high spirits too.

Our hotel was on a steep central street with a distinctly European air, with cheerful cafés and lit-up shops. That it was nearly Christmas and festooned with decorations reinforced this impression; the prayer flags flying from the tops of Buddhist temples strangely not detracting at all. A giant Christmas tree dripping baubles stood snugly in the lobby of our charming hotel, so snugly there was barely room to squeeze past and up the ornate stairs to our rooms.

While I would have gladly stayed in with a bowl of soup and a good book, having brought Dame Daphne's *Rebecca* along for a reread, we had agreed to mingle that night, and so strolled out together into the Himalayan cold. Ushered into a sumptuous Nepalese restaurant, twinkling with lanterns, and with low, food-laden tables, we were generously plied with a fiery rice wine that took us to a nightclub after. On a fact-finding mission, stated Thom, our researcher, and Gopal happily agreed, so we jostled with lots of young people for snatches of yelled conversations over an insistent beat. If we came away with any facts at all, by the next morning, they were a pleasant blur.

It was my escape in the morning from the team and the hotel that really exhilarated. I found a café a stone's throw away, with a brightly painted shop front and flowering plants, in which I could sip my hot chocolate and contemplate my day. As a bonus, for breakfast they served momos, my favourite snack! Being a reasonably adventurous eater, I picked a platter of yak, finding it a stronger than expected flavour but delicious with its hot garlicky sauce.

Kathmandu is a colourful little city you can wander around for hours, up and down the hilly, winding lanes that are occasionally suggestive of small cities in India or China, the giants on either side, but with a quirky vibe of its own. True to its multiple personalities, the wide avenues leading to the royal palace were quiet, as were the large swanky casinos, though filled to the gills with foreign tourists who murmured in sotto voce. But the rest of the city – the lanes, cafés, and public spaces, in which locals congregated – was abuzz with raucous, curious, but friendly voices. They were to be found in the vibrant marketplaces, with their colourful stalls selling all manner of things spilling through the narrow lanes. They sold rucksacks, raiment, spices, travel books, and glass-studded brass lamps. Often from the same shop!

The most surreal offerings in Kathmandu's markets, and so many that it choked every shack, were jesters' hats. Not only were they piled high on the stalls, with shopkeepers wearing them jauntily, many more could be seen adorning the heads of tourists and revellers in the city. It was bizarre and made great footage, but it mystified us too, becoming a story in its own right. We were told that a large consignment of jesters' hats had been ordered from France for fans to wear to the FIFA World Cup. Gazillions were manufactured and shipped out of Nepal, practically propping up their economy for a while. The surplus stayed at home however, and continued to swamp Nepalese markets for years. Especially as visitors to the markets picked them up as mementos long after the World Cup. 'Why jesters' hats?' I'd asked. The shopkeepers had laughed and said they didn't know, but wasn't it a brilliant comment on our funny old world?

Their sales patter blended with the tapping of feet, of market-goers going up and down the narrow streets, or staying put to hang out and have chai, maybe even smoke the occasional spliff. There were many tourists doing just that, even more than wore jesters' hats. Togged out in clothes, hair, and totems from an array of cultures, they were often in Nepal looking for inspiration. As they went in and out through the porous borders, drugs changed hands, and sometimes, far more often in those days when it was understood less and managed worse, AIDS was passed along too. Like the pandemic we are living through now, there was much panic, little knowledge, and even less hope. But there was also a special stigma attached to AIDS, because it was thought to be something that didn't affect ordinary people. It afflicted only wayward souls, it was believed, who deserved the fate that befell them and had to be pushed to the margins of society.

We were quietly tipped off about little clinics, rehabs, and squats for the disowned, addicted, and ailing. They were difficult places to find and even harder to countenance: down back alleys, behind other more 'respectable' facades, and often literally in the shadows. The people we met there were naturally keen to conceal their identities even as they wanted their stories to be heard. 'We have become wraiths; treated like we don't exist, except as a problem.'

At the same time, there was another shadow stretching across Nepal – a climate disaster in the Himalayas that would haunt future generations, and not just in their part of the world. In pursuit of that story, we travelled farther up to Pokhra. In this vale of glassy green waters and deeper green trees climbing the dizzying slopes of the mountains that cocooned it, we stopped at the lake to take it all in, talking to smiling bystanders with their vividly patterned caps – daubs of red and orange against the verdant backdrop. We listened to the stories of their beautiful yet changing world with wonder and alarm, making plans to return. But we had an engagement that evening we hadn't been able to wriggle out of.

If in Kathmandu we'd holed up in a European style chalet, charming but not especially grand or posh, our billet in Pokhra was quite another matter. Driving through extensive grounds and up the sweeping driveway, we were stunned to see the palace that awaited us, with liveried staff spilling out to help us with our sparse luggage. A blond man in an expensive suit, redolent of yesteryears' Hollywood, rushed out to greet us too. Guided down plush corridors to our vast and elegant rooms, we felt like we'd been dropped, headfirst and dazed, into a big-budget film production. More Bollywood perhaps than Hollywood, judging by the dinner that followed – a sumptuous alfresco meal and musical soirée in a courtyard swirling with silks and flowers, lights and dancers, aromas and sparkling chatter.

With the morning came reality, and our mission in the mountains, as we drove to the small outposts of conservationists fighting the onslaught of pollution, tourism, and deforestation. I left with much to mull over, not least a sense of displacement I could relate to. It had begun to dawn on me that as 'happening' as my high-flying job was, and at such a young age, it wasn't what I wanted. Deciding to shun chirpy company and opulent entertainment that night, I stole away with a small packet of momos to Lake Pokhra's serene shores. Like in the hotel the night before, music was being made, but without the 'jhinchak' of our music channel parlance. Instead, the full-throated, heartfelt a cappella renditions of boatmen rang through the night to convince me, 'Leave it all behind.' But if I didn't want this life, with its professional success, celebrity interviews, occasional luxuries, and a thousand superficial friendships, what did I want?

As I walked back to the hotel that night, I considered how deep connections were hard to come by, especially in the world I inhabited whose denizens seemed to skim over everything, flitting from person to person, from cause to cause, never delving deep. I wanted deep. I wanted a simpler life, revolving around the people and passions that really mattered to me. People who 'got' me, even just the one special someone, either seeing past my atypicality, or connecting because it was there. I hadn't got even a whiff of such an individual yet.

Waking the next morning in my posh, nearly-all-glass hotel bedroom, I watched the sun rise from behind the highest mountains in the world and knew there was hope. For me and my dream of finding my people, for all those lost souls I'd met in the course of our filming in Nepal, and for the world. Hope, but no guarantees of happy endings unless we acted on our intentions. It was the end of our trip and nearly the end of the millennium, and I made a promise to myself to trust my instincts and strive harder to find the life I desired. Then one day, when some of those promises had been met, to come back to this land of epiphanies, to its green lakes and greener mountains, and this gorgeous room in the clouds, with those I love. Less than a year later, I found myself in the quiet northern English city of Sheffield, with the rolling green Yorkshire Dales at its door, with the intention to walk, read, write, and make a home.

Pause for Thought: A Plan for All Seasons

With such a lot of travelling these days, we need to take much into consideration before we head out on our journeys. Where do we want to go, and why? The Greek islands for your honeymoon? Disneyland with the children? Or that Egypt trip you've been planning forever for your fiftieth birthday? Excellent plans all. But can we do 'em? Not before you've weathered the dull but deadly serious business of sorting out budget, transport, accommodation, currency, vaccinations, and travel docs.

But before you organize anything else, what you need to determine is – when. When's best? That obviously differs from person to person. Far too often, it isn't even up to you. It can depend on when you get leave from work, or the children have their school holidays. Both of which can be at inconvenient times of the year, and don't even synchronize often. British schools break for the summer in August, when summer's been and gone. And in India, it's usually in May, when you have to stay indoors or be sautéed. 'When' could equally be that time of year when flight and train tickets are best priced. But that never coincides with school holidays, when transport companies blithely hike their fares to milk families on their rare breaks in a year.

215

Hitting on the right 'when' can be crucial too, if it's good weather you demand from your vacay. Yet, if you can't even control your 'when', can you expect the weather on your trip to behave? *We* have achieved a measure of control over it, taking the weather with us wherever we go (like the band Crowded House advised in the nineties). Our sway over the weather doesn't extend to type however, so what we take abroad with us is rain. Nippy English rain.

Talking of weather, we must discuss whether. Whether we should travel long distance at all any more, taking the impending climate disaster and the ravages of long-haul travel on the planet into consideration. We undoubtedly need to cut back, and if this pandemic has taught us anything, it is that we can. Yet, in a world where families are far-flung, it would not be possible to dispense with long-distance trips altogether. We can all tighten our travelling belts instead, wandering less, but more wisely, focusing on those trips that really matter to us. We can also endeavour to enjoy what we have more. Far more. On holiday and at home.

The vicissitudes of the 'when' ensure you never really have enough say in what you pack, see, or do. Festivities and activities are largely seasonal around the world, and if you land up in Lapland after Christmas, you might just see Santa having an extended doze. Rajasthan in the summer might prove too hot for sightseeing, and Moscow in the winter mired in snow. And yet, what if you do find yourself in the wrong place at the wrong time? If it's not a crime caper you've stumbled into, have no fear – there'll be plenty to do! With an open mind and a receptive nature, you'll have fun whatever the season, vagaries of the weather, and activities on offer. Couldn't make it to New Orleans in time for Mardi Gras? There's historic architecture, scrumptious Creole cuisine, and foot-tapping jazz to which you can surrender.

Getting the 'when' right – with schools, careers, budgets, climactic interference, bureaucratic snarls, and life's many surprises – becomes a feat of superhuman strategizing. Time it right and you will be rewarded with uplifting experiences well worth the sometimes gruelling trek. Fairy-tale Cotswold villages in the verdant English countryside don't look half as spiffy behind sheets of wintry rain. And a flooded Kolkata is not the best time to sample its legendary street food, because you aren't the only microbe swimming in its stew. Yet, time it wrong and it still completes you. You learn to weather the storms, and while you're about it, have tons of fun. And food.

25

France in Summer

Le Grand Prix

The road trip: an extended journey in a motor vehicle, according to the Merriam-Webster dictionary.

If you've seen enough American movies, then you know about its joys. Maybe even its drawbacks. They are either very glamorous pitfalls like Brad Pitt asking to come along for the ride when all you want is me-time. Or they are so unlikely, e.g., carjacked by aliens, that you figure they couldn't happen to you. But the joys and horrors of a road trip are very real, just different from how Hollywood depicts them. Road trips intensify the pros and cons of travel because you aren't being ferried around by train, plane, or coach. You are driving, or part of a group doing so, and in control of where you go, when to stop, and with whom you interact. But when things go wrong, to fix that is up to you. For that reason, road trips are seen as more individual and freewheeling. Consequently, everything experienced must be more deeply felt too. Whilst the latter is true, the former is not.

Hark back to my first road trip of any magnitude, in my preteens from Delhi to Rajasthan and back, and the sorry details I regaled you with in an earlier chapter, and you'll see why it can be style-cramping, spirit-constraining, and anything but individual. After that first attempt at a road trip, I've been on plenty others in India, and many more in Britain, but taking care not to attempt too great a distance or stew in enforced proximity for too long. It's not just about time in the car, on a road trip you find yourself inextricably entwined with your tripfellas as if attached with an umbilical cord. Not only have you travelled there together, you are then expected to spend every single second with them! So when another road trip was broached, this time covering a vast distance, from one country to another, I hesitated. Because the first rule of road trips is, of course, not to factor in more time together than you think you can stomach. But it was France we were talking about, France of the fabulous art, delectable food, verdant vineyards, and abundant joie de vivre; how could I possibly say 'non'?

The plan was to travel from Britain to France by car, with only the stretch through the English Channel, the undersea tunnel called The Chunnel, on a train, but still sitting in our vehicle. An earlier shot at a French road trip, from Britain to Brittany, was beset with babies and teething problems (not necessarily connected), and we hadn't tried again till our children were a decade older – eight and ten years of age. But luckily for us, what we'd remembered of France was not the dissonance of that first trip, but the delights it hinted at. Despite the rented farmhouse turning out be in the middle of an industrial estate, and the towns and villages within driving distance bleak and shuttered, we'd seen enough of France on that trip to know it promised so much more.

Paris, a few years later, though not on a road trip, confirmed this feeling many times over – that France was the perfect holiday for history connoisseurs, with a literary bent, and a penchant for good food and gorgeous surroundings. As much as we all loved Paris, quite possibly our favourite capital city, we would not be returning there on our road trip this time. Instead, we planned to explore historic Normandy, the husband, son, daughter, and I, savouring it at our own pace and according to our own lights.

Stopping over in Dover before our Channel crossing, the sun was out and our spirits high. Jokes were cracked and songs sung, even as far too many jujubes were consumed. The crossing was as smooth as the ride down to the coast, and breezing along on the other side, on France's wide, orderly motorways, we tried to remember why it had seemed so much trouble the last time round. But of course, our children were full-fledged card-carrying Sen-Handleys now, whereas on our trip to Brittany many years ago, one hadn't even been born, and the other was three months old. Travelling with a baby presented problems we'd never encountered before, as did so much else on that trip. Our grown-up children, however, were a different kettle of bouillabaisse – entertaining and adventurous. Hence, even time spent on the road became enjoyable, as we eagerly coasted to our destination. The second rule of road trips then would be to know your roadies.

Considering we didn't know nearly enough of the French language, we got to Beuzeville without mishap, finding ourselves on a quiet farm lane thick with trees and birdsong. The Tudor-beamed flat at the end of the track was bijou but welcoming, tucked under the thatched eaves of a converted barn, with tiny but comfortable bedrooms, tinier still bathrooms, a surprisingly modern living space, and a balcony with an ornate iron bench from which we could watch both the life of the farm and the moods of the weather. Whilst sunshine greeted us most days that week, even flambé-ing us lightly on some, the clouds rolled in often enough, washing the land with fine rain. We even had a night of tumultuous thunderstorms, which cleared up serendipitously the morning after, just as we headed out that day. Equally magically before supper each evening, the drizzle that returned with us to our rented apartment after a long day's exploration would vaporize as we set the barbecue up for one of our many scrumptious alfresco meals that week. Dinners made from local greens, fish, and meat from busy markets, with delicate desserts from the neighbourhood patisserie, and more varieties of aromatic cheese than you can shake a freshly baked French baton at! Our nearest town not only provided a surfeit of gastronomic delights, but the butcher's patter, the baker's songs, and the charms of the cheesemonger were also a draw!

A short drive from our cosy retreat for the week was the seaside town of Trouville-sur-Mer. Magnificently sunlit on the day we visited, it was abuzz with daytrippers in search of treasure at its famous pan-European market. Basking in the sun, we examined pretty trinkets, bright, wide-brimmed sunhats, and fly swatters. The last of which we bought, owing to the preponderance of inquisitive cows around our barn, endearingly sticking their nose into our activities, but sadly leaving flies behind. It was the range of food on offer, however, that sang to us and we were soon sampling uniquely Gallic ice cream flavours ('Escargot, s'il vous plait'), squirrelling away creamy cheeses for breakfast the next day, and carrying home a large pail of Spanish paella over bumpy country lanes, whose tender prawns and spicy chorizo in sumptuous saffron rice was well worth the effort.

The next morning we were back in the car heading for picturesque Honfleur. The drive was hilly, cool and green, and intriguing for the homes you inadvertently looked into as you passed, so narrow were the roads, and crowded with hill-hugging houses. Finding an expanse of silver sand before we got there, we felt compelled to stop. Settling on the sand under big, blue skies, as the children played with an abandoned beach ball, we made inroads into our large purchase of local cheese, even as we decided to save our stash of rainbow coloured light-as-air macaroons for the next destination. Pacing your nibbles on the road is the third rule of successful road trips, or you could emerge several pounds heavier.

Honfleur had a picture-perfect harbour, with thronged restaurants, cavernous galleries of art, and even a fun fair clustered around it. Tables at the bistros were hard to find, although we joked about having a natural right to one in a quaint pub named after Robin Hood, coming as we did from the same neck of the Sherwoods. So we sauntered instead, dipping into the cheerful shops, buying further sweet treats, especially from the chocolatiers, and becoming transfixed by their ancient town hall in luminous stone.

But it was Bayeux in which we found ourselves lost in the past. The famous Bayeux tapestry, the story of the Norman conquest of Britain in 1066 sown onto a seventy-metre length of linen by a medieval sisterhood of nuns, enthralled the children, as they picked out the colourful, quirky details, querying each one. 'Why does Harold look so pleased to have an arrow in his eye?' and 'I have counted seven pigs already. Were there many pigs at the Battle of Hastings?' They asked each other, then us, and finally, William the Conqueror. Wooden old William sitting in his throne looking dour wasn't more help than us ('Despite the fact that he'd actually been there!' exclaimed our little girl rolling her eyes), but the museum had plenty of information to impart, and could have engaged us all day had we time. Grand cathedrals and churches awaited us, as did food shopping in the lanes, so we moved on, bumping into the biggest band of Bengalis I'd seen anywhere in France. 'No?! From Jodhpur Park too?', 'Dhakuria-r oi chicken roll-er dokan-e kheyechhen nishchoi?'...

With its old houses, charming central marketplace, little bistros, and elegant but bijou boutiques, compact Beuvron-en-Auge was prettier still. Despite its quaint toy-town feel, with its brightly painted doors, and seaside amusements, it had its uses too, so we browsed in the curiosity shops to find gifts for friends, the cider shop to get ourselves some very French breuvage (not that different from 'beverage', see? You pick words up soon enough), finishing with mouth-watering chocolat crêpes at la petite crêperie.

On we went to large, bustling Le Havre, down motorways as featureless but more efficient than their British counterparts. On a quest to discover more about the great Impressionist Claude Monet who had lived and worked there in his youth, we arrived at a cosmopolitan conurbation unlike any of the towns and villages we'd happened upon till then. Alongside the very Gallic bistros and boutiques were Indian restaurants called Namasty India and Le New Delhi, Chinese supermarkets, and vivid graffiti from a famous Thai street artist. An ornate Gothic cathedral that reminded us of our awestruck tour of Notre Dame in Paris offered a soothing break for our sore feet, before we headed out to the port from which mushroomed an eye-catching sculpture. This looming Lego arch couldn't but catch the eye, so high did it soar above the ships and the city.

Yet, Monet himself proved elusive till we got to Giverny and his gloriously blossoming estate. The drive down was pleasant, with a stop to see an eccentric house on a bridge – an ancient toll house, but many other things over the years as well. The plan was to get away from the hurly-burly by immersing ourselves in the tranquil beauty of Monet's art, but his home was a riot of colours, style, and unfortunately, tourists. Which meant standing in long, slow-moving lines till we got to the house and garden we'd come all that way to see. Between the backs of the gawkers, we stole glimpses of an elegant house, a truly impressive collection of art including his own fabulous works, and a garden that was heaven on earth (but a crowded one).

His quirky, colourful sense of style was especially apparent in his sunny-yellow and cobalt-blue chequered kitchen. Weaving across the monochromatic floor, through the vivid pottery and furnishings, I noticed for the first time that we were being tailed. A starchily-dressed woman was tiptoeing after us, her stare drilling into our backs. 'Hello?' I turned to ask, but she kept her unwavering gaze fixed on the children as she advanced. Anxious, as any parent would be, I grasped their hands firmly, and alerting my husband, escaped into the rambling grounds. In Monet's luxuriant yet meticulously manicured gardens, his famous paintings have been recreated. We walked through the floral arches of *The Artist's Garden*, leaned over the green Japanese footbridge of *The Water-Lily Pond* to glimpse lotuses glistening upon it, and without tourists hemming us in, we ran like the wind through the field of red poppies from his famed 1873 painting. Here, in his gardens where his canvasses have been brought to life, we could more than metaphorically lose ourselves in the colours and patterns of his paintings, and we did. But with my children close beside me, till it was time to go. 'Did one of your kids drop this?' the security guard asked us on our way out, holding up an unfamiliar scarlet scarf. 'A lady left it for you.'

The enchantment only grew as our Normandy trip progressed, and we pressed South to the island of Mont-Saint-Michel. Starting that grey day feeling sick reminded me of the highlight of our first road trip to France: the storming of Châteaubriant. It hadn't been the sunniest day then either, nor the most exciting, but as soon as we drove up to the old hall, I was gripped by its Gothic ambience. The 1537 murder of a former mistress of the French king by her husband – the lord of the castle – had let loose its malevolent spirits, who to this day walk its ramparts at midnight in the autumn. It was summer however, despite the murky skies, and we would not get to see the macabre sight the townspeople swore by. But the fine Chateaubriand steaks and dainty crème brûlée we had at a café there that night made up for it.

The weather on the way to Mont-Saint-Michel, an island mired in sandy marshes with an imposing hilltop abbey, was similarly overcast and off-putting. On the road, an intense pain overtook me. I'd suffered from endometriosis for a few years, a condition without a cure for the millions of women afflicted by it, and attacks of pain were both severe and without warning. 'Do you want to turn back?' asked my husband, concerned. 'No,' I forced through my fog of pain, not wanting to disappoint the children. 'We must carry on. I'll be fine.' Downing a painkiller, I pumped up the music – Bruce Springsteen for the worst pains – and drifted. Songs on the road are a great distraction for fretting children and out-of-sorts adults alike. Even pets are known to be soothed by it. Alongside the jellybeans, medicine pouch, and first aid kit, we always have music on our road trips – on the car radio, CDs, and our own fund of songs, to croon together as we jolt along! The fourth rule of road trips that is then.

Riding up to the legendary isle, the setting for so many books and movies, we saw only shifting mists over marshlands stretching out to sea. The lowering clouds of that murky morning reinforced this ominous impression, but we had arrived, and we pushed on. Then, in a flash of dazzling light, we were rewarded. The clouds raced away, pursued by the swirling mists, revealing a gilded world before us; beckoning from a gleaming hill was a castle with gold-tipped turrets. But more captivating still was the expression on the faces of our children, watching transfixed as the fairy-tale island floated into view. 'This is the castle from Disney's *Tangled*!' our daughter cried out, even as our son murmured happily about having finally found the Count of Monte Cristo's stomping ground. My pain forgotten, I laughingly joined in, 'You're absolutely right. It is all of those, and earlier still, it is the island of Avalon the troubadours sung about.'

Walking up the cobbled lane that winds to the abbey at the top, we peered into delis, patisseries, curiosity shops, and makeshift museums. On the stone steps at the base of the towering abbey, the atmosphere turned less touristy, though there were hundreds making their way up. Yet, awestruck by the sight before them, they had quietened down. The air felt purer too, the sky a gleaming blue, with the streaming turret-top banners seen from afar playing hide and seek in the cotton-ball clouds. We began our tour in the depths of the abbey, in which mouldered a dark dungeon with tall columns of great girth. Perfect for a game of tag, the kids decided, and they were lost to us momentarily as they skipped in and out of the shadows. We worked our way up the many floors of the abbey, gazing at stained glass windows, elegant stonework, and the many historic artefacts, till we came upon the jewel in its crown – its sweeping terrace-top view.

All around us were the vast marshes melding with an infinite, silver sea. Closer at hand were the bronzed hills tumbling to the sometimes turbulent coast. Calm when we saw it, it allowed us to spy the tiny Roman-era cottage still clinging to its shores. We stopped at a church near the causeway from the island to share our ham and cheese baguettes with circling seagulls, before walking back to our car on the mainland. We couldn't help looking back however, so enchanting was the sight of the island in the mists, swirls of which were beginning to wrap around it once more. Distracted in this way, we ended our day unwittingly photobombing a wedding party, captured for posterity sheepishly entangled with the bride's gargantuan train and the groom's many drunken friends.

Yet for me, the coastal town of Étretat was even more thrilling. Parking in neighbouring woodlands, we'd scoffed a lunch of red bell peppers, artisan bread, salami and cheese, before wandering into the jaunty holiday town with its Tudor-beamed houses and colourful shops. We bought bright pottery, and even cheerier hats (adorned with cats' ears for the girl and a bobbing sailboat for the boy), but it wasn't till we arrived on the seafront that we were truly blown away. And not just by the gusty sea winds. In my many years of beachcombing, I'd never seen anything like the prospect that materialized before us. Buffeted by the gale and in danger of losing our new hats, the view kept us rooted to the spot.

On either side of us loomed green and gold cliffs. Giant rock limbs reached down to the sea floor from each, framing the scene like a picture: the wildest, most primeval work of art. In the ceaseless sea before us, curling, climbing aquamarine waves rose and dropped, leaving us untouched, as if restrained by their rock encasing. More than a painting, it was like being inside a snow globe, sloshing with sea-green water, whipped winds, and the smell of seaweed, with something preternatural emerging from the mix. Surreal, even scary, but breathtakingly beautiful. Passing a plaque on the pier on our way back that said Monet had spent months here capturing the astounding beauty of this sea, we were in no doubt why he'd try.

We, on the other hand, aspired to nothing more than a meal nonpareil to finish our fabulous French road trip. Asking around, we found that the petite town of Pont-l'Évêque not only did a delectable homegrown cheese, but had some fine restaurants too. So it was that we stumbled upon the Chef's Hat or the Auberge de la Touques for our last meal in France. Finding a table, it soon became obvious that the minimal French we'd survived on would not be enough to communicate with our waitress that night. Our transactions would have to be conducted almost entirely in the international language of mime. Flailing about madly, we ordered an array of gastronomic wonders, to each item of which the waitress expressed her delight. Yet, when a dinner of duck l'orange, dauphinoise potatoes with braised asparagus, and chocolat profiteroles arrived, we weren't at all startled. They weren't what we'd ordered, but they were a delicious surprise, and the most fitting way to end our grande French getaway.

Which brings us to the fifth and final rule of road trips: go where the road takes you. C'est la vie, after all, oui?

26

Cambridge in Early Spring
The Queen's Gambit

Cambridge, Wordsworth's city of 'turrets and pinnacles in answering files', of scholars and spires and cobbled miles, of academic dreams and drinking teens, and poets and pubs and punting (flat-bottomed-boat-steering) teams, lured us into its beautiful, blue-stockinged embrace one spring. We'd had a draining winter, with record snows in the UK bringing an extra dollop of winter blues, and the usual stresses and strains that come with parenting two rambunctious toddlers. So we hatched this plan of rejuvenating ourselves with a trip to this 2000-year-old, yet young and vibrant, city. We planned to drink deeply from its font of youth, to soak up its energetic vibe.

As it happened, we did find our youth there – in the back of our car. Not quite how you'd imagine either. There they were, our two toddlers strapped in safely and along for the ride. Of course, we hadn't forgotten they were there, but as they'd unexpectedly dozed off, we'd allowed ourselves the luxury of daydreaming of a reckless weekend without responsibilities. A student weekend. A punting weekend. What we got wasn't fast and furious but brushed by magic. The kind of experience you can only have with young 'uns untouched by cynicism, who know anything is possible and make you believe.

Our Cambridge sojourn started with a gentle stroll down cobbled walks. Each walk led to a different, historic college. A ramble through the oldest one, Peterhouse (c. 1284), led us to Pembroke, a century younger but dripping atmosphere. And icicles on this cold, clammy day. Arriving in March, we had hoped for the perfect spring break with flowers blooming and birds on the wing. We were gifted instead, in the wild beauty of Pembroke, with its frost-laced shrubs and rain-shiny old stone walls, a scene straight out of Narnia. Is this what C.S. Lewis saw when he taught at Magdalene?

A winding walk away is Trinity College, established by Henry VIII, just weeks before he died in 1547. There was something here for all of us, from the heavenly choral music in its beautiful sixteenth-century chapel with life-sized statues of alumni like Newton looking on, to the largest and most picturesque courtyard in Oxbridge for the kids to gambol in.

But it was Queens' that touched our hearts. Not as grand or as beautiful as some of the others, there is a feminine aura about it that makes it more ... welcoming. The clue's in the name, of course, as it was set up by two queens of England: Margaret of Anjou, the French 'she-wolf', and the fairest of them all, Queen Elizabeth Woodville, progenitor of the Tudors. In their lifetime, they were at war over England, but in death, they are together forever at Queens'. Yet, it isn't just its history that makes it a warmer, more likeable place. The gatekeepers, a pair of clucking, helpful women instead of the stony, bowler-hatted men we encountered everywhere else, reinforced the impression, as did the indulgent students who smilingly watched our children frolic on their lawns.

You can't, of course, visit Cambridge without blowing by King's College or St John's. The former dwarfs the rest for sheer scale and Gothic splendour. Five kings of England presided over its building, and Salman Rushdie spent many an uncontroversial student year here. To St John's, with its glorious gateway, goes the credit for having kicked off (literally, during a scuffle with Oxford undergraduates in 1829) the venerable tradition of the Oxbridge boat race.

As evening descended, the contrast between the swinging single life and the wholesome family life became sharper. The householder has a single, staid drink instead of a binge, followed by a hearty meal at a child-friendly restaurant rather than a night on the prowl. Then it's tucking in time for the kiddies, while we sink exhausted on to the nearest available comfy surface and have a warming cuppa. Outside, in student digs and nightclubs around town, rave parties rage into the wee hours.

Sunday morning dawned bright and early for us. Bright with frost on our windows and ankle-deep snow on the ground. We'd promised to go punting, and so, off we trudged. To Magdalene for this most Oxbridgian of activities, with the crunch of snow underneath to remind us how completely uncomfortable it was going to be. But the children's exhortations ensured we didn't turn back.

Described by Rupert Brooke thus, 'The stream mysterious glides beneath, green as a dream and deep as death ... To smell the thrilling-sweet and rotten, unforgettable, unforgotten.' Our own punting experience turned out to be just as mysterious, and as unforgettable. It started off swimmingly with the kids snug in their tartan blankets, and their father, the keen amateur photographer clicking away. Whilst I, happy to have a moment to sit back, watched the world glide by.

But then the kids spotted something of immense interest floating by, and as any serious Winnie-the-Pooh fan knows, short twigs swimming along together is a sure sign that somebody up there, on one of Cambridge's many bridges, was having an impossibly good time. In the blink of a cuddly bear's eye, the blankets were off and they were hanging from the side of the boat (though in our vice-like grip), shouting ecstatically, 'Pooh sticks, Mommy, pooh sticks!' As the punt wobbled ever-so-slightly, an elderly tourist grew wobblier still, 'Poo? Is there poo in ze water, hein?' When our attempts to shush our excited children and reassure our finicky fellow passenger came to naught, we were forced to disembark at Queens' Mathematical Bridge to restore equilibrium to the Cam.

Feeling like the founding fathers of Cambridge, kicked out of Oxford for disturbing the peace, we were making our cold way up the bank when a woman with a regal air sailed towards us from the enveloping fog to offer the shivering children warm drinks and shawls. Startled by this gesture, it took us a moment to thank her and offer to pay, only to find she had vanished into the mists rushing in from the river. Not that surprising on such a pea-soupy day, but as we hastened to our hotel, our faith in humanity restored, I couldn't help thinking with my fanciful hat firmly jammed on, that our encounter had been with no ordinary mortal. Indeed, no mortal at all. Recalling the portraits in Queens' College's ancient hall, I was tickled by the idea that our Good Samaritan might have been Queen Elizabeth Woodville herself, bereaved mother of the princes in the tower, forever mourning her lost boys and anxious to help other children in distress.

Cambridge on an unexpectedly wintry March weekend may not have been at its best, but what a story our spirited experience would make!

27

Britain in Winter
Christmas Chronicles

'We were on tiptoe, craning to get a better look. Around us, thousands jostled for the best view of the dazzling Christmas tableau on the first storey of Anson's, the biggest department store in a prosperous eighties' Manila. It was the most important time of the year for a devout Roman Catholic Philippines, and there were church bells pealing everywhere. But as this was a country that knew how to have fun too, there was glitz and bonhomie. A visit to see Anson's automated Christmas display was part of our family's annual ritual. In the middle of the crush, one balmy evening in 1983, were three Indians – my diminutive mother, four-year-old sister, and me. We watched in wonder as nimble elves danced to the rousing sounds of an illuminated choir of angels, in a swirl of fake snow. Then a cheer went up as a blur of red and gold jingled into the midst of the tableau. Santa had arrived – rotund, rubicund, and jolly – with his retinue of frolicking reindeer. Nothing could be more exciting to two little girls (and one woman in touch with her inner child), but the day was waning, and with a festive dinner waiting for us at home, we had no choice but to tear ourselves away from that magical spectacle—'

I interrupted my story as my children's attention was momentarily caught by a vendor in elf costume rolling a trolley full of seasonal goodies past us. On a frosty morning in early December, we were on the Christmas Special train from Nottingham to Lincoln for the biggest Christmas fair in Europe. A month ago, we had decided to take our kids there to enjoy a classic British Christmas. The togged up train put us in the Yuletide mood, and my story of Christmases past bolstered the festive feeling. 'Tell us more,' said my young son.

'We got home to the delights of a traditional Filipino Christmas dinner – honey-and-cinnamon glazed ham, chicken adobo, and sticky-sweet coconut lumpias. Gathered around our modest but twinkling tree after dinner, my parents caught up on their reading while my sister and I kept a close eye on the gifts beneath the tree. It would not be the gifts that disappeared however, but that whole way of life. Sooner than we could have imagined.'

'What happened, Mommy?' our little girl asked, alarmed. Glimpsing the soaring spires of Lincoln Cathedral, I pushed ahead with my story. 'There was a revolution brewing and my father didn't think it safe to remain in the Philippines with a young family. We returned to Kolkata where, despite my mother's best efforts, recreating those fabulous Filipino Christmases proved impossible. We would scour Gariahat unsuccessfully for Christmas trees and baubles as New Market felt a tad distant. And while Park Street was very merry come Christmas, the rest of Kolkata didn't necessarily follow suit. Still, my mother was a great believer in festive fun, whatever its antecedents, so Christmas in our home continued to be celebrated with delicious food, good company, and even carol singing (lusty renditions from the family, with hesitant interpolations from our guests). But the splendour was missing, and so was Santa with his capering crew. I felt like I might never experience a perfect Christmas again.'

I wrapped up my account as we walked into Lincoln's central square. Though their brows had furrowed at my tale, the children were instantly swept up in the thrill of the Christmas fete. The fair swamped Lincoln, but the city's cynosure with its ancient cathedral with Tudor luminaries buried within remained relatively serene. Parliament was held here in the fourteenth century, and *The Da Vinci Code* filmed in its hallowed halls more recently. Just across the cobbled square was Lincoln Castle, a drab museum with a magnificent facade. Walking past the ruined abbey and rows of pastel-coloured homes, we stopped for a one-sided natter with the statue of Lincoln's favourite son, Victorian poet Tennyson. But the kids were quick to remind us why we were there. So, we plunged into the packed heart of the fair, dipping into festive stalls, picking up Swedish baubles, German cake, and quick gulps of Irish cream (with hot cocoa for the kids) to keep warm on that icy day. In a narrow snicket, we were ambushed by ladies in Regency dress who arm-twisted us into buying their cinnamon-spiced nuts, cooing over the children all the while. And then our little girl spotted the most magical carousel shimmering at the end of the street. 'Looook,' she breathed awestruck, pointing to the antique carriages, each of which was a red-and-gold sleigh. 'A ride, m'lady?' Their father chuckled, hoisting both children in.

The following weekend, we cantered to majestic Chatsworth House in the Derbyshire Dales. The Duke of Devonshire's estate is considered the grandest in Britain, perfectly placed in green, rolling Derbyshire. It is also believed to be the mansion on which Jane Austen based Darcy's estate, Pemberley. With its extensive landscaped gardens, immense orangery bursting with every kind of flora, Elizabethan hunting lodge, and ornate Italian fountains (their waters frozen into sparkling crystal shards on that bright winter's day), it was nothing short of dazzling. Four-and-a-half centuries ago, Mary, Queen of Scots, was incarcerated here by her jailor and lover, the Earl of Shrewsbury. Our own Warren Hastings' Chatsworth connection is evident in the rooms full of purloined oriental treasure.

Pulling a wry face, we made our way to the spectacular entrance hall. There, the children gazed in wonder at the magnificence of the massive Christmas tree, and the sweep of the red-carpeted stairs with glittering tinsel and holly twined around each balustrade. Chatsworth was celebrating a Georgian Christmas, and everything from furnishings to festive decor, to the sheets of music at the grand piano, was in keeping with the theme. Even the dinner laid out in the vast dining hall, ablaze with baroque candelabras and crystal chandeliers, was Georgian.

In their tempting farm shop, there were festal favourites on sale – cranberry sauce and chestnuts, sage and sausage stuffing for the Christmas turkey, fruity festive cake and mince pies, bottles of eggnog and mulled wine. And to the children's delight, shelf upon shelf of elf, snowman, and Santa-shaped chocolates. Returning to the sedan with more goodies than we could consume in one Christmas, we found ourselves embroiled in a snowball fight with a group of children, ducking and diving behind the frost-laced bushes of the icy car park. Relieved to have held on to our wobbling pile of luscious purchases through the boisterous snow battle, we went home sopping but pleased as punch with our hoard.

But Christmas isn't complete for kids without a session with Santa. For this, we travelled to the splendidly shabby Calke Abbey in Leicestershire. That year, they were playing on their gone-to-seed wartime look. The intriguingly melancholy dining room was arranged to look as if a bombing raid had sent the family scurrying to the cellars, leaving their festive dinner untouched. The dust-covered furniture was askew, the shutters off their hinges, and the walls had damp patches so elaborate they looked like art. Up the hill to the quiet family church was a joyful trail of traditional decorations. The freezing winter wind loped up the rise with us, ringing the bells in the trees, rocking the little wooden sleighs that led to the church door. We found Santa in the Victorian stables, smelling of damp and hay. Yet, so warm were Father Christmas and his helpers with their genial chatter and thoughtful presents, that the odour and bone-rattling cold were quickly forgotten. We all agreed that Calke Abbey with its heart-warming conviviality easily outdid grander places in festive cheer.

No Yuletide outing can finish without food, so we braved more mud and biting wind to join the bustle in the large, beamed barn. Alongside handcrafted wreaths, sweets and spirits, were tables piled high with Calke's famous reindeer pies. Finding a warm corner, we were ready to tuck in when we noticed our children's reluctance. 'Is Santa's reindeer in there?' our son asked anxiously. Despite our swift reassurance that these were made from farm-reared reindeer, and that Santa's squad with its gift-transporting duties was far too important to ever become pie, they were clearly not convinced.

We couldn't let the festivities end on that sombre note, so we plumped for an impromptu trip to Edinburgh to see the year out. Edinburgh is an elegant city with grand old architecture, mouth-watering seafood, and the wettest, windiest weather in the British Isles. In the depths of winter, we knew it would not be comfortable, but the annual Christmas market and Hogmanay festival did promise colour, excitement, and the perfect end to our classic British Christmas. Bundled up in our warmest woollies, we jostled with thousands for a safe perch on Edinburgh Castle's medieval walls just as the torchlight procession began. To the beat of drums and pipes marched Vikings, Romans, and men in Tartan kilts, the national costume of Scotland. There were even a few 'Bravehearts' in blue face paint. As night fell, Edinburgh lit up like an enormous firecracker. In fact, there were colossal crackers going off everywhere, the noise mingling with the cacophonous warbling of drunken revellers. Manoeuvring our way out of the crowd, we returned to our room where a tasty dinner and bottle of bubbly awaited.

Just before midnight, with the kids asleep, my husband and I stood at the Victorian sash windows and listened to the countdown from the square, clinking glasses as the clock struck twelve and up went the cheer. I had found the perfect Christmas I'd been looking for since I left the Philippines.

28

Kolkata in the Monsoon

Homecoming Joys

The crows had started cawing in the milky light of dawn. The noises of the house waking reached my drowsy ears shortly after. The bustle grew outside the half-open door of my old bedroom where I lay snugly cocooned in the mosquito net with my children. I was a guest in my ancestral home with no chores to perform for a change. Breakfast was being made, the newspapers had arrived, and the laundry had magically come back clean.

Coaxed out of bed with a cup of sweet tea, I found hot jalebis, segments of tropical fruit, and a luxuriously cheesy omelette in the dining room. Stuffing myself in the fond hope that we'd soon get out and work it off, I discovered it was nearly lunchtime. The only sensible course of action was to wait for the chholar dal, potoler dolma, kosha mangsho, and shorshe illish. Satiated, I fought off the impulse to indulge in the other Kolkata favourite – the never-ending siesta – because the kids had had enough of the easy life. They were all set to explore their mother's jostling, crumbling city. So we struck out into the great beyond. Into Kolkata.

At the turn of the century, I had left these shores for adventures in Blighty. Thirteen years later, I was back on a journey of rediscovery. It would also be an introduction to my former home for my young children who were growing up a world away. In the wettest six weeks of the year, I hoped to show them all that I had found to love in two decades of exploring the city. I was excited but anxious. Kolkata's charms are not the obvious kind. Its beauty is in the sounds and tastes, and in the way they make you feel.

I felt nothing but love for my city until I was six. I loved its mildly nippy winters. Warmed by the sun on the terrace, on our winter break from school, my cousins and I would help with the day's cooking by shelling bright green peas and defuzzing baby carrots. We would eat more of those tiny green globes and tender orange sticks than we put in the pot. For our 'hard work', we were rewarded with plump raisins, oranges, and notun gurer sandesh. Then there were trips to Alipore Zoo with my mother's clan. The overwhelming animal smell of the place would fade amidst the joys of watching wondrous creatures, and tucking into Tutti Frutti ice cream in the mellow midday sun.

But closest to my heart is a monsoon memory of my sprightly, large-hearted great-grandfather wading through knee-deep water to entertain me on a dreary afternoon.

As soon as he arrived, there would be magic in the air. We would make puppets out of eggshells and scraps, stage shows with our delicate marionettes from behind the dining room curtains, write comic poems, read tales of adventure, and end the evening with philosophical discussions on Feluda, Tintin, or the Little Prince, while sharing a slab of chocolate.

'Did Feluda like chocolate?' I would ask, trusting him to know everything.

'They ALL loved chocolate, like all intrepid souls.' He twinkled, meaning him and me as well, of course.

The next five years were spent in the Philippines. In the gleaming capital of Manila, I developed new interests. I loved the sea and the balmy weather. I discovered Nancy Drew, Judy Blume, and Bruce Springsteen. The family I had left behind, especially my beloved great-grandfather, were never far from my mind, but time and distance opened up a gulf between me and my old city. When we returned to Kolkata, my great-grandfather was no more, and the unalloyed love I had for my hometown died as well. The summers felt searing, the monsoons relentless, and the winters biting compared to the tropical climate I had embraced.

But loving Kolkata is like learning to swim: you never forget how. In the years after our return, at first grudgingly and then with growing enthusiasm, I rediscovered my city. I went on morning walks round Dhakuria Lake with my cousins while the air was still fresh and the grass dewy. My grandmother's magnificent pot roasts on Sundays were worth moving country for. A couple of times a month would find us in central Kolkata, sampling its cosmopolitan delights –

from posh patisseries to roadside shacks selling meaty Mughlai 'rolls', to tiny shops in New Market flogging trendy togs, and cavernous old cinema halls showing Hollywood blockbusters. There was also the newly instituted Nandan screening cerebral cinema alongside brightly lit new bookstores where you could, for the first time, sit and browse. These things sustained me through high school and university. When, as a television journalist, I began delving into Kolkata's cultural riches for our award-winning show, I fell in love with my city all over again. Now I was back for more with my youthful Ingrej brigade.

With another enormous lunch under our belts, and a pause in the rains, we dashed out for the adventures I had promised them. We headed for the open spaces the children would enjoy. At Dhakuria Lake, we watched passionate games of soggy cricket, traipsed through green, dripping Safari Park looking for a dry swing, ending up, as always, at the Calcutta Rowing Club. The clubs of Kolkata, set up by the British as their refuge from the heat, grime, and 'natives', have become the watering holes of the city's middle class. They give Calcuttans one more reason to get together in a salubrious spot, argue vociferously, and then make up over excellent grub. I have fond early memories of the CRC, of its children's Christmas parties with drawing competitions on flowering lawns, tables laden with cake, and strangely slim Santas. The Anderson Club was another childhood haunt. Emerging shivering from an evening swim to warm ourselves with piping hot lentil soup was a weekly ritual. To these clubs we returned so the children could run like the wind, rummage in bushes for lizards, finding kittens instead, and dig into tubs of Two-in-One ice cream.

The next day, we went farther in our search for great open spaces. Victoria Memorial in its oasis of green was a breath of fresh air after the choking, cacophonous traffic on the way there. Victoria was her usual regal self. Designed by William Emerson a century ago in a hotchpotch of architectural styles (Indo-Saracen Revivalist with Mughal and Greco-Roman), it was no less elegant for it. If it soothed me to gaze upon its vast marble facade after the chaos we had just endured, it pleased the kids as much to spot statues of stately lions, trumpeting angels, warlike generals, and Victoria in voluminous robes.

'Aren't they hot wearing those big coats in Kolkata, Mommy?' my three-year-old daughter asked. I told them it was called 'colonialism' and that their English father, flying in that night, would explain what it meant.

The children would have spent all day galumphing about on the damp grass, watching kites (of the avian variety) wheel overhead and attempting to pet mangy dogs, had a gusty squall not sent us scurrying in. Inside the dark, cavernous halls, they found other raptures. Shadows and echoes became playmates as they pored over centuries-old cutlasses, hoary cannons, and the dramatic paintings of tigers. Rain couldn't dampen their day.

Back outside, avoiding the schools of sad donkeys and their manically persistent handlers, we made our way to Kolkata's 'lungs' – The Maidan. Despite the sodden ground, there were swarms of people there with the same idea, of escaping the reek and rumpus of the more congested parts of the city. We wandered past ancient trams, football scrums, and vendors advertising their wares in sing-song voices. We stood where the Kolkata Boi Mela or Book Fair had been held till the High Court moved it to the Eastern Metropolitan Bypass in 2009 for environmental reasons. It had been an annual pilgrimage for many of us, equally devoted to books and food. For the Book Fair had been endless lines of book stalls punctuated with pungent shacks peddling fish fry, chicken roll, and bhars – tiny terracotta tubs – of tea. And people, shoulder to shoulder, toe upon stubbed toe, passionately going about their business of choosing books and refreshments.

Streaked with pink, the sky reminded me we should return home before the mosquitoes came out to feast on young flesh, slathered though the children were in insect repellent. Their father was due to arrive within hours.

He got a day to recover from jetlag before we went exploring again. We headed for Park Street, the home of my television years and my favourite part of the city. At the end of the street is a darkly romantic eighteenth-century cemetery, with lichen-stained headstones and the occasional giggle-inducing epitaph ('Here lies Lisbeth Brewster, undone by a portion of pineapple' or something to that effect). Lost amongst the almost entirely European, generally Gothic, memorials is the tomb of Indologist Sir William Jones. His is a distinctly Hindu edifice with a central dome and black basalt carvings – an affirmation of his love for India. I was glad to have found it amongst the shadows and rivulets of the rain-washed graveyard, but a discernible shiver running down our little girl's spine had us herding them back into the sunshine.

Our next stop was just off Park Street, where my elegant all-girls' college appeared as it always had, untouched by the hurly-burly around it on Middleton Row. Run by Catholic nuns from 1912, Loreto College had the calm of a nunnery and the sheen of a finishing school for well-heeled women. As I showed my family around the deserted college that holiday, I could hear the whispered stories, shared laughter, and occasional heartbreak of generations of girls in its corridors and classrooms. They were reminders of our many tiny rebellions, secret revels, and brushes with the young men who waited beyond the high walls for a glimpse of us at the end of each day. Right next to Loreto House and College is the tranquil St Thomas' Church. There before Loreto, but with the same stillness, which is occasionally shattered by the outside world. When Mother Teresa was laid in state there in 1997, the world streamed in through its doors, disrupting its distinctive hush. A year later, I was responsible for disturbing the peace while shooting inside for MTV. But on that afternoon with my children, it was bathed in the serene glow that the blazing sun emerging after a spot of rain confers on Kolkata.

We'd become so unused to peace in my polyphonic city, we needed a pick-me-up after our sombre tour of cemeteries, churches, and cloistered colleges. At Flurys, arguably the finest tea room in town, we found pastries, savouries, and that gorgeous coffee and ice cream concoction called coffee Sprungli. Since opening its doors in 1927, Flurys has collected a large and determined clientele, my family amongst them. There was never a trip to central Kolkata that did not involve a visit to Flurys. As I admired the plush new interiors fitted after a fire in 2010, the kids took it upon themselves to pick the pastries we planned to purchase.

'Another six of these?' the man behind the counter checked with my five-year-old son, while frantically running his eyes over the shop in search of his parents. I sidled up to my enthusiastically nodding son to scotch that transaction: 'We'll have ten of them!'

With one day left to see the sights, we decided to go off the beaten track. We arrived at the Temple of a Million Mirrors in Maniktalla as the sun set, gilding every square of its cut-glass facade. In a city with lots of character but little awe-inspiring beauty, this was a place I particularly wanted to show my family, and not just at any time of the day. The nineteenth-century Pareshnath Jain Complex, a group of four temples adorned with mirrored mosaics and stained glass, can appear kitschy in daylight, but at sunset, it's dazzling. Its twilit glow exudes a spirituality that touches even the non-believer. So we breathed it in – the sparkle, the serenity, and the faintly scented air.

But it was dinner that promised to be heaven. Dropped off at the entrance to the dark, labyrinthine lanes of the Tibetan Quarter in central Kolkata, we went looking for a diminutive eatery with divine momos I remembered from fifteen years ago. Yet, nearly every identical tiny room, crammed with tables, had delectable smells wafting out. With little hope of finding my old haunt, we decided to eat at the busiest, brightest one. As I prepared to pop my first proper Tibetan momo in years into my mouth, our little girl asked earnestly if she could skip the 'boring soup'. Startled into dropping my precious morsel, I was relieved to find that neither child had taken a sip out of their finger bowls.

Our last week was devoted to friends and family we wouldn't see again for months. Alongside pujos and parties at their homes, were tea, digestives, and dalmut (or shingaras, if it wasn't raining) on the balcony with my parents. Lunches of mushoor dal, mocha chingri, and mishti doi with the whole family round the table. Wrapping up each satisfyingly slow day with late-night addas after the kids had fallen asleep.

The day before we left, I turned forty. As friends from different chapters of my life, most of whom I hadn't seen in over a decade, gathered on Calcutta Rowing Club's twinkling lawns, I realized how fortunate I was to have brought them together. Past exploits were recounted with warmth and laughter, absent friends remembered, and the city's future discussed with hope and despair in equal measure. Blowing out the candles on my cake, I made a wish to keep coming back to the city of my birth for as long as I could.

Final Pause: No Place Like Home ...
However Many Places
That Might Be

'We can't wait to come and see you all!' their Didou and Dadu, my parents, said in unison as the video chat came to an end. 'We've missed you!' chorused the children in reply. Their father, reading in the background, with his new reading glasses perched professorially on the end of his sharp nose, cheerily waved to demonstrate how much he too was hoping to see them. Then, with a reverberating woof from our dog Luna, who'd developed an impressive baritone bark in her three years, our twice-weekly virtual adda ended.

We were wrapping up not just our last chat of the year with my faraway parents, whom we hadn't seen in the flesh for two years, but also the loose ends of this pandemic year. In this time, not only had travel ground to a halt, concert halls and theatres had shut down to stop the spread of the deadly virus. What that had also stopped – a minor tragedy amongst the many terrible ones this year – was the premiere of the 200-performer-strong show I'd co-written, for which my parents had planned to travel the 5,000 miles to Britain. Fortunately, it is back on for 2022, as is their expedition. Yet, not having undertaken any major journeys since touring

France and England with us eight years ago, after which my father had gone through a period of illness, they confessed to feeling 'norbore' about long distance travel now in their seventies. Their beloved grandchildren, daughter, and son-in-law, waiting at the end of their long trek, could not banish the bureaucratic hassles and physical rigours of the journey they would inevitably have to face. But, we all agreed, it would be worthwhile at journey's end. 'You'll be coming home.' I beamed at them.

There really isn't any other journey like a homecoming. Having been on many jaunts of adventure and discovery, if I had to pick the excursions that meant the most to me, they would have to be the ones in which I come home. These are not only my trips to my ancestral home in Kolkata, which we did annually, and hope to resume in a not-too-distant future that is pandemic-free. Nor are they limited to the ones in which I return to my husband and children gratefully, after the occasional unaccompanied journey. The latter can be exciting, but they inevitably begin to feel too long, and then I'm glad to scoot home to my family. I'm never happier than when I'm heading home. That melting joy and feeling of fulfilment that attend every homecoming are amongst the finest feelings on this earth.

But every now and then, they also happen at destinations that are brand-spanking-new to me. In an unknown land, I could be struck by this feeling in a joyful instant, enhanced by the presence of my family. Or in the pursuit of a passion, whilst experiencing an epiphany. 'Ohhh,' pipes up my ten-year-old daughter, having taken all this in. 'Like in the Latin

Quarter in Paris.' Just like that, I assure her. Celebrating my thirty-ninth birthday in its tangled lanes, with my parents, husband and kids, we happily watched the Parisian crowds of many ethnicities, buying and selling in the bijou boutiques, or eating, as we were in an Iranian canteen, suffused with the aroma of fresh food cooking. I had felt similarly when wandering on my own through the cobbled lanes of old Zurich, amongst fine art, old bookstores, artisan chocolates, and people who allowed me to be just me. These places, if only momentarily, were home too, by virtue of how they made me feel. At ease, complete, and in harmony with the world.

You are home if you love what you're doing, and the people you are with. My travels, relationships, interests, and indeed, my whole life, has been about finding home. But in its many avatars. 'Home is where the heart is' may sound trite, but is not only true, it isn't at odds with a yen for travel and adventures that feed the soul. 'Home is that feeling of being whole,' our twelve-year-old son sagely adds, 'and of filling up a hole, but with your favourite things, not putty.' I beam at them to say I get it, and now may I finish writing? I have one last paragraph to write, I tell them, and then my third book is complete.

'Dinner, m'love,' at just that moment, my husband pops his head into our library, where the children and I are writing or reading. 'I've made your favourite seafood linguini.' Putting the laptop away, I herd the children to the kitchen. The night is still young and my book's final line will keep.

Acknowledgements

I have been fortunate to have found a willing audience for my travel stories over the years; so some of these I've had the pleasure of relating before, in similar or different shape, in a range of publications. Most of the stories in this book, however, that I've felt compelled to tell, are newly dredged from old memories, dished up with love and mischief. My aim was to tell you stories you could relate to, nick ideas from for your own trips, titter over, and be entertained. So, there is little striving after scholarly verisimilitude, though the occasional fact may have crept in.

Writing this book through a pandemic, mostly in lockdown, and at a time when I have discovered I'm autistic and have always been, has meant that quiet reflection has been my companion through this transformative year, and fewer people have left a mark on it than with my previous two books. But those that have, have left a strong imprint, even as they've supported it to its completion. To them I would like to say a huge thank you: my editors at HarperCollins, my husband Stephen Handley, my two children, both my parents, and our dog. All of whom are a large part of this book whether I have allowed them to chew on it, or not.

Sources

As mentioned earlier, some of the chapters in this book were carried in various publications before. Here's a list acknowledging each:

Chapter 1 titled 'Kolkata Durga Pujas: Armed and Marvellous', in *National Geographic*, 2017.

Chapter 2 titled 'London: Night at the Museum', in Livemint, 2018.

Chapter 3 titled 'Gotham: Batman's Lair', in Livemint, 2019.

Chapter 6 titled 'Amsterdam: Sex, Drugs, and Sunflowers', in *National Geographic*, 2013.

Chapter 7 titled 'Zurich: Moo-ving On', in *Café Dissensus*, 2018.

Chapter 8 titled 'Sheffield: Nerves of Steel', in *National Geographic*, 2013.

Chapter 9 titled 'Nottingham: Second Chances in Sherwood', in *The Hindu*, 2014.

Chapter 13 titled 'England and Wales: The Game Is Afoot', in *National Geographic*, 2014.

Chapter 14 titled 'Dorset: Four Go Off in a Caravan', in *National Geographic*, 2013.

Chapter 15 titled 'Haworth: Wuthering Heights', in *National Geographic*, 2018.

Chapter 16 titled 'Wales: Train to the Top', in *National Geographic*, 2018.

Chapter 17 titled 'Disneyland, Paris: Never Never Land', in *National Geographic*, 2015.

Chapter 23 titled 'London: Orf with Their 'Eads', in *National Geographic*, 2014.

Chapter 26 titled 'Cambridge in Early Spring: The Queen's Gambit', in Millennium Post, 2013.

Chapter 27 titled 'Britain in Winter: Christmas Chronicles', in *National Geographic*, 2013.

Chapter 28 titled 'Kolkata in the Monsoon: Homecoming Joys', in *National Geographic*, 2014.

About the Author

Shreya Sen-Handley is the author of *Memoirs of My Body* (2017), which won the Best Nonfiction Book of the year at the NWS Writing Awards 2018, and the short-story collection *Strange* (2019). A Welsh National Opera librettist and the first South Asian woman to write international opera, she has collaborated with WNO on their film series *Creating Change* in 2020, and a 200-performer multicultural opera *Migrations* touring Britain in 2022. Her play *Quiet* was staged in London by Tara Theatre in 2021.

Her short stories and poetry, published, broadcast, and shortlisted for prizes in India, Britain and Australia, also spearheaded a British national campaign against hate crimes in 2020.

Shreya teaches creative writing at various institutions, including the University of Cambridge. She is also a columnist and illustrator. She lives with her husband, two children, and a dog, in Sherwood Forest, England.